Yale Romanic Studies, Second Series, 26

Critical Fictions
The Literary Criticism of Jean-Paul Sartre

Joseph Halpern

New Haven and London, Yale University Press, 1976

Published with assistance from
the Louis Stern Memorial Fund.

Library of Congress catalog card number: 75-18172
International standard book number: 0-300-01943-2

Designed by John O. C. McCrillis
and set in IBM Baskerville Selectric type.
Printed in the United States of America by
The Murray Printing Co., Forge Village, Massachusetts.

Published in Great Britain, Europe, and Africa by
Yale University Press, Ltd., London.
Distributed in Latin America by Kaiman & Polon,
Inc., New York City; in Australasia by Book & Film
Services, Artarmon, N.S.W., Australia; in India
by UBS Publishers' Distributors Pvt., Ltd., Delhi;
in Japan by John Weatherhill, Inc., Tokyo.

To my parents

Art, of its essence, is opposed to that which exists; its task is neither to glorify nor to explain; its value is one of terrorism; it is a weapon against traditional values and morality; it is aggressive, challenging, destructive; it leads established society to deny itself through the medium of the culture which it demands. This is the great lesson of de Sade and the true surrealists.

SARTRE

Contents

Acknowledgments

I would like to thank Professors Marc Bertrand and Raymond Giraud of Stanford, Victor Brombert of Princeton, and Paul de Man of Yale, all of whom read this book at one stage or another in its preparation, and whose advice and conversation were invaluable. I am especially indebted to Robert G. Cohn of Stanford, under whose personal and intellectual guidance this study was conceived and developed. I am grateful to *Diacritics* for permission to reprint in revised form articles from the issues of Winter 1972 (vol. 2, no. 4, pp. 60-63) and Fall 1973 ("From Flaubert to Mallarmé: 'The Knights of Nothingness,' " vol. 3, no. 3, pp. 14-17), and to the Council on the Humanities at Yale for a grant that aided me in completing the manuscript.

Introduction

The literary criticism of Jean-Paul Sartre today can be most clearly understood in the light of his entire critical production: the early phenomenological works and the latest Marxist-existentialist writings are mutually illuminating. Sartre's current ideas on the creative process develop from problems he first considered forty years ago, and the formidable intellectual armament progressively built up within his criticism, the distance traveled in methodology, complements a remarkable stability of themes and imagery.

In one of his earliest essays Sartre first established a mythology of the philosopher as hero, as prophet and artist. In an article on Husserl's concept of intentionality—the idea that all consciousness is consciousness *of* something—he attacked the traditional academic philosophies of his day. His neo-Kantian professors in the French universities taught what Sartre designates as the "alimentary" and "digestive" philosophy of idealism, according to which the world is wholly constituted by the activity of consciousness. "The Spider-Spirit drew things into its web, covered them with a white slaver and slowly swallowed them, reduced them to its own substance. . . . The mighty ridges of the world were worn away by these diligent diastases: assimilation, unification, identification. In vain did the simplest and the plainest among us seek something solid, something, in a word, that was not of the spirit; all they came across was a soft and ever so distinguished mist: themselves."[1]

1. "Une idée fondamentale de la phénoménologie de Husserl: l'intentionalité," *Situations 1* (Paris: Gallimard, 1947), pp. 29-32. Page references follow in the text; the translations are my own for all of *Situations 1*.

Elsewhere, Sartre has dismissed such idealism as an "illusion of immanence," [2] which holds that my image of another is like a tiny homunculus existing somewhere within my consciousness. To the philosophy of immanence, or "being," Sartre opposes a philosophy of transcendence, or "doing," which begins by locating objects outside of man. The essay on intentionality was written in Berlin in the early 1930s, in the enthusiasm of Sartre's first direct encounter with German phenomenology, and in it Sartre berates the "bourgeois, mechanistic psychologisms" of his fellow countrymen in acid tones. All valid writing, to Sartre, functions as both negation and construction; his vision of the artist and the philosopher in this essay expresses just such a dialectical origin. Husserl, he claims, has pulled thinking man back from the pinkly sensual charms of the "effeminate philosophy [*la philosophie douillette*] of immanence, where everything is done by compromise, protoplasmic exchanges, by a tepid cellular chemistry" (31), to throw him naked onto the cold, comfortless path of heroes: "On the open road, with danger on all sides, beneath a blinding light . . . Husserl has restored the world of artists and prophets: dreadful, hostile, menacing" (31-32).

The artist-prophet, philosopher-hero is a masculine figure, form-giver, hard and erect, "thing among things, man among men" (32). He lives, however, in a soft, clinging, damp, muddy, and glutinous world, a "moist gastric intimacy," "a stinking brine of the spirit"; his primary recourse, as taught to him by Husserl, is a form of violent action that tears him from contemplative retreat, an angular, vertiginous, and immediately experiential knowledge that is both flight and explosion, confrontation and pene-

2. See *L'Imaginaire* (Paris: Gallimard, 1940). In *L'Etre et le Néant* (Paris: Gallimard, 1943), he speaks of the "substantialist" illusion, p. 643.

tration. The adventure of consciousness is a flight from an
enclosing fluid, a stomach, a caressing womb, from a shut-
in, overheated room, where all the blinds are drawn, from
formlessness, from intimacy and self-love ("in vain would
we seek . . . like a child who kisses his own shoulder, the
caresses and fondlings of our intimate selves" [32]); it is a
flight of the child from the mother, and an explosion
toward the hardness of things: a refusal of passivity, of dependence, of "relative being," of femininity. In the way
that Rimbaud admired the rough workmen of his town
and saw in them the incarnation of masculinity, so Sartre
begins to think of the new philosopher and of himself as
among the simplest and plainest of men, so he begins to
exorcise all that is feminine in his world, to oppose himself
to the aesthete, to "nos raffinés": "And there we are, de-
livered from Proust" (32).

The obsessive sanctification of the masculine and the
denigration of the gastric-feminine are overwhelming in the
few short pages of the essay on Husserl. The overwrought
tone of the essay is startling for a philosophic discussion,
and it is precisely this tone that is the key and the impetus
of the argument. The choice of vocabulary, with the heavy
load of sensuality it bears, is essential to the essay. For instance, we may puzzle over the justification of a phrase
like "la philosophie douillette de l'immanence," until we
happen on the following remarks in *Saint Genet:*

> When [Genet] speaks of Darling's *derrière douillet*
> ["downy behind"] we can be sure that he does not
> couple these words for the truth or beauty of the as-
> semblage, but for its power of suggestion. . . . And
> what about *douillet?* Where does its *meaning* begin?
> Where does its signification end? The fleshy blossom-
> ing of the diphthong suggests a kind of big, heavy, wet,
> silky flower; the trim, dainty flexional ending evokes

the coy grace of a fop. Darling drapes himself in his behind *comme dans une douillette* ["as in a quilted wrap"]. The word conveys the thing; it is the thing itself. Are we so far from poetry?[3]

At the root of Sartre's critical thought we find poetry, at the origins of his philosophy a passionate outpouring of imagination. The opposition of male and female, the schematized landscape of the essay on Husserl, is not accidental to the thought, nor is it posterior. The word *douillette,* draped in heavy folds of flaccid effeminateness, is not a careless addition; it delivers exactly the concept and nuance Sartre intends. Sartre's sensitivity to sexual dichotomies and to the conception of writing as a heroic act constitutes in part the *parti pris* of his criticism and underlies, as would an original choice, his judgment and understanding of literature from his earliest essays.

Sartre has provided us with at least two reductive models for these patterns of thought: his autobiography and his earliest major philosophical works. At the end of *L'Etre et le Néant,* in a dazzlingly bizarre section entitled "Quality as a revelation of Being," Sartre proposes a "psychoanalysis of things," which will explain the human meaning of objects by a "method of objective interpretation that does not suppose any previous reference to the subject [the *I*] " (766).[4] That is, "man, being transcendence, establishes the meaningful by his very coming into the world, and the meaningful because of the very structure of transcendence is a reference to other transcendents which can be inter-

3. *Saint Genet, Actor and Martyr,* trans. Bernard Frechtman (New York: Braziller, 1963), p. 492. Originally published as *Saint Genet, Comédien et martyr* by Gallimard in 1952.

4. *Being and Nothingness,* trans. Hazel E. Barnes (New York: Washington Square Press, 1953).

preted without recourse to the subjectivity which has established it. . . . A psychoanalysis of *things* and of their *matter* ought above all to be concerned with establishing the way in which each thing is the *objective* symbol of being and of the relation of human reality to this being" (767-68). If the psychologist wants to understand why someone likes lobsters and hates oysters, he must understand the objective meanings of lobsters and oysters and the origin of those meanings, the way in which they symbolize being.

For Sartre, each man's "original choice" of himself is a choice of values, tastes, and preferences; it embodies an understanding of the world and a particular orientation toward the world. We each choose to "be" in a certain way, and our relation to objects, our attempt to "appropriate" the world through things, is symbolic of our total being. To understand ourselves and to understand others, we must elucidate "immediate and concrete existential categories" of things, the "existential significance" of objects (that is, the manner in which they reveal being). For example, in considering a child's fascination with holes, Sartre rejects any explanation of this phenomenon in terms of the anal character of infant sexuality, or prenatal shock, etc. The hole is symbolic of a mode of being, it is a nothingness-to-be-filled, and the child's relationship with it depends on its ontological meaning. Only from here can one move on to the realm of sexuality.

Nonetheless, what is important for us is that one *can* move on to sexuality. "We do not deny that we should discover afterwards a whole sexual symbolism in nature, but it is a secondary and reducible stratum, which supposes first a psychoanalysis of presexual structures" (768). Granted, Sartre's literary criticism, founded in ontological principles not always explicit in his text, can be traced to what appear to be more fundamental levels, and its preoccupation with sexual categorization is partially derivative.[5] But even if sexuality is *in theory* a secondary matter, still there is for Sartre a "whole sexual symbolism in nature," and it is a strangely personal one at that: "The obscenity of the feminine sex is that of everything which 'gapes open' . . . it is with his flesh that the child stops up the hole and the hole, before all sexual specification, is an obscene expectation, an appeal to the flesh" (782). The "viscous," an existential category Sartre establishes as "the agony of water," a repulsive quality of being that corresponds to the "dawning triumph of the solid over the liquid" (774), is particularly crucial to our argument. The viscous is docile: "It is a soft, yielding action, *a moist and feminine sucking,* it lives obscurely under my fingers, and I sense it like a dizziness; it draws me to it as the bottom of a precipice might draw me

5. Restated in *Un Théâtre de Situations* (Paris: Gallimard [Idées], 1973), pp. 162-63: ". . . je ne suis pas convaincu que la base de l'activité humaine soit sexuelle. Qu'elle le soit ou non, je ne crois pas que l'infrastructure du besoin sexuel réapparaisse intacte dans la superstructure de la personnalité. Elle peut réapparaître mais à un niveau complètement nouveau."

Sexual categorization and symbolization are secondary according to Sartre; just so, his literary criticism should be dealt with at one remove from the ontological givens of his system. I shall not discuss Sartre's criticism in terms of the search for being (as does George Bauer in *Sartre and the Artist* [Chicago: University of Chicago Press, 1969]), but in terms of its correlative, the search for masculinity. This focus is consequent, perhaps, to the responsive-to-the-text nature of literary criticism—itself a "derivative" activity—in which the techniques, though offshoots of a metaphysics, in Sartre's famous phrase, bring us back more directly to a human questioning of relationships within society, to biography and autobiography—at least for literary criticism as Sartre practices it: a measuring of the self against another. To discuss Sartre's criticism only in the light of *L'Etre et le Néant* and the *Critique de la raison dialectique* would be to distort the tone of Sartre's criticism, which by and large (with some exceptions—the essay on Ponge, for example) avoids recourse to any reduction beyond the human. In *Baudelaire* Sartre does not talk of the desire of the *pour-soi* to be also *en-soi* but of the poet's desire to be simultaneously subject and object.

. . . it clings to me like a leech . . . it is a trap . . . a sickly sweet, *feminine* revenge which will be symbolized on another level by the quality 'sugary.' . . . To touch the viscous is to risk being dissolved in viscosity" (776–78; my italics). The viscous is that which most specifically threatens to engulf the male.

The obsession with the artist as hero and the basis for that obsession form the major subjects of Sartre's autobiographical work, *Les Mots*[6]. There he discusses at length the sources of his obsession: the need of the child Jean-Paul to feel himself necessary in the world, to produce a work of massive proportions to legitimize himself and to mirror himself as indispensably present, undeniably real. In *Les Mots* the conception Sartre presents of "justified" and "unjustified" existence reflects elements of social class and ontological status, but it is formulated principally in terms of sexuality.

Sartre conceives of his childhood self as unnecessary in the world because his existence, in his own eyes, was feminine. As he sees it, within the world of his family's play-acting, Jean-Paul's only real function was to give the adults their cues. His character, his name, his "truth" were in their hands; Jean-Paul gives himself to them promiscuously and guiltily, knowing uneasily that he does not really count and that he is being used. His is what Sartre terms a "relative being"; that is, his existence is dependent on an ontologically prior existence, his meaning is the sum of the opinions of others, his status is that of a fetish. His acts, therefore, turn into empty posturings, his life is ceremonial theatre, and his role is only to please and seduce others.

---

6. Gallimard, 1964. Page references following in the text refer to the translation by Bernard Frechtman, *The Words* (New York: Braziller, 1964). I have made some minor changes in translations here and elsewhere. I take "obsession" in the sense of a reiterated structure; I do not mean that Sartre is "obsessed" in any pathological sense.

It is especially his grandfather, a handsome, patriarchal figure with a flowing beard, half-Jehovah, half-Victor Hugo, whom he must conquer. "We would put on a full act with a hundred varied sketches: the flirtation, the quickly dispelled misunderstandings, the good-humored teasing and petty scolding, the lover's chagrin, the tender pretense of mystery, and the passion; we would imagine our love being thwarted so as to have the joy of triumphing in the end. I was at times imperious, but caprices could not mask my exquisite sensibility" (26). The supposedly model grandson is, as Sartre sees him, a spoiled impostor, an imaginary and "false" child (as Genet is considered a "false" child), impressionable, yielding, feminine clay, "indefinite in flesh and blood," useless and superfluous. His mother dressed him at this age as a girl, cherished his blond curls, and would have wished him to be a girl, but the best she could do was to invest him with "the sex of angels, indeterminate, but feminine around the edges." "I was *nothing:* an ineffaceable transparency" (90). "Feminized by maternal tenderness, dulled by the absence of the stern Moses who had begotten me, puffed with pride by my grandfather's adoration, I was a pure object" (112).

The unnecessary existence is understood as feminine and transparent; the apparently necessary existence is masculine, solid, and free. The kind of man who seems to be needed, who is seen to be missing when absent, is a proprietor, a bourgeois who possesses property and his own self down to the "granitelike mass of his tastes" consistently, permanently, materially. To exist so essentially means to continue the father's work; it means being a man among men: "A few days ago, in a restaurant, the owner's son, a little seven-year-old, cried out to the cashier: 'When my father's not here, *I'm* the boss!' There's a man for you! At his age, I was nobody's master and nothing belonged to

me. . . . Worldly possessions reflect to their owner what
he is; they taught me what I was not. I *was not* substantial
or permanent, I *was not* the future continuer of my father's
work, I *was not* necessary to the production of steel. In
short, I had no soul" (88).

To be the phenomenologist, to be the Husserlian hero,
also means for Sartre to be a man, not in the sense of the
self-justified male existence of the property owner, but in
a way that measures equally in its masculinity. For the
young Jean-Paul writing is a mandate from the father; the
one time his maternal grandfather replaces his father, he
becomes Moses dictating the law, delivering to the child his
vocation. Jean-Paul will write, and in a poetic language he
first envisages as forbidden to women. The Sartrian hero as
artist-philosopher must tear himself away from the ordered,
protecting, motherly world of the false child to throw himself into the adult male's frightening, sharp, nude reality of
things, the remorseless, unkind world of indifferent nature.
It is a world Jean-Paul does not know. "I later heard anti-
Semites reproach Jews any number of times with not
knowing the lessons and silence of nature; I would answer,
'In that case, I'm more Jewish than they.' In vain would I
seek within me the prickly memories and sweet unreason
of a country childhood. I never tilled the soil or hunted for
nests. I did not gather herbs or throw stones at birds" (49).
It is also a world that frightens him: "I was afraid of water,
afraid of crabs and trees" (151). Jean-Paul is a false child
partly because his world is theatre, but also because the
reality of nature has been stolen from him. For the land-
owner there is order in nature; his existence is necessary as
part of that order, his fields and houses mirror his own
stable self-image and reflect what he is; and his masculinity
is thereby defined. But the "fatherless orphan" Jean-Paul
must become a man by facing an orderless, formless world

filled with water, crabs, and trees to which no meaning has been assigned, a world of sexually orchestrated guilt and accusation. In many ways, this is the impulse and the function of literature for him: to become a man in a shapeless universe, Sartre will seek for direction and definition of self through writing, that is, through words.

In Sartre's imaginative writing the quest for the self has always been an ambivalent one. For Mathieu in *Les Chemins de la liberté* and for Orestes in *Les Mouches,* the quest for self and the quest for freedom have their dangers as well as their attraction. The bad faith of both Mathieu and Orestes is generally recognized; lucid introspection may entail a turning away from others. The search for identity through writing itself is even more ambivalent. In an early attempt to establish a phenomenological theory of imagination Sartre portrayed the imaginative act as double-edged.[7] What he said is that to imagine is to negate the real—which is to establish the freedom of consciousness—and therefore the act of imagining stands as the model of man's liberty and transcendence. At the same time, to imagine is to flee reality, to imprison consciousness in an "infantile," "imperious," "factitious," "slackened," "impoverished," and "debased" mode. To write a novel is the act of a hero. To write a novel is the act of a coward. Sartre's choices lie within this framework.

The effects of this nexus of sexual-heroic schemata are quite clear in Sartre's fiction, where intellectual structure is most obviously intertwined with the imaginative impulse. In Sartre's novels and plays the dominant themes and images, the decor and landscape, and the repeating linguistic patterns are all directly influenced by Sartre's dislike

7. *L'Imaginaire.* See particularly the conclusion.

for—or at least his concern with—the feminine element within him. As Suzanne Lilar has pointed out, Sartre's antipathy for the feminine gives birth to an identification of the feminine principle with evil. The essential dualism of the masculine and the feminine in Sartre's works can be expressed in a metaphysics of purity and impurity: "D'un côté le pur, le vif, le léger, le net, le sec, le froid, le dur, le ferme, le stérile, le minéral; de l'autre l'impur, le trouble, le flou, l'épais, le pesant, l'informe, le traînant, l'humide, le tiède, le mou, le gluant, le fertile, le vivant et la foule de leurs synonymes." [8] The world of woman is the world of viscosity; woman is acquiescence and quicksand; as Lilar puts it, she corrupts, she contaminates, she compromises. Femininity is a threatening trap for the male because it is not understood as being restricted only to the female sex. It is rather a mode of being, an ontological choice, that is open to all.

Lilar uses Sartre's distinction between the masculine and the feminine as a guideline to his fiction, in which one finds abundant observations on the feminine way of thinking, acting, feeling, and imagining—ways that are always suspect, always tempting the male. In Sartre's novels the "veulerie" of feminine relationships is often opposed to the "netteté" of masculine ones, and healthy masculine decisiveness and self-sufficiency are contrasted to feminine deceit and entanglement. Lilar shows that in *Les Chemins de la liberté* Sartre proves himself far more attracted to the evidently asexual, adolescent, almost androgynous type that Ivich represents than he is to the heavily sexual presence of Marcelle or the voracious sexuality of Lola. In contrast, she evokes the austerity and asceticism of Brunet as an ideal of Sartrian virility. One could easily continue her

8. *A propos de Sartre et de l'amour* (Paris: Grasset, 1967), p. 21.

argument, as other critics have done, to include Roquentin
in *La Nausée*, who rises from the feminine mud of Bouville
to split the night, and whose project is to write prose "as
beautiful and hard as steel," or Orestes, for whom the death
of his mother means liberation and who pictures himself as
an axe, a wedge come to split Argos and to "take" his
sister.

What has not been shown as clearly is the extension of
these patterns into Sartre's critical writing. Perhaps because of the immense and complex intellectual structure of
Sartre's criticism, the immediacy of his tastes and preferences has seemed obscured. Nonetheless, those preferences
subtend and balance his thought throughout his work. Unlike Benjamin Suhl, in his book on Sartre's criticism,[9] I do
not intend to examine the philosophical origins and logic
of Sartre's critical ideas. Rather, I am postulating a wholeness in Sartre and trying to build a synthetic (and fictional,
perhaps) construct of the impulses expressed in his criticism
by drawing forth certain patterns and repetitions, certain
variations on an original theme, that have a specific urgency
and weighting not always inherent in the subject matter.

Sartre has spoken of *L'Idiot de la famille*, his latest work
on Flaubert, as a novel, and of his Flaubert as a partly invented character. The same remarks can readily be applied
to the rest of his criticism, most particularly to *Baudelaire*
and *Saint Genet;* Sartre's criticism is essentially creative, as
much so as any other form of his art. The paradigm for
Sartre's critical work, which has remained a constant attempt to imagine the creative act, is Roquentin's vision in
La Nausée of the birth of the jazz tune that almost saves
him. It is this, rather than Roquentin's documentary at-

9. *Jean-Paul Sartre: The Philosopher as a Literary Critic* (New York: Columbia University Press, 1971).

tempt to recreate the imaginary Marquis de Rollebon, that has borne the most fruit in Sartre's work. Roquentin's strictures about his own critical fabulation ("Ça s'est passé comme ça. Comme ça ou autrement, mais peu importe.") are echoed in both *Saint Genet* ("Cela s'est passé ainsi ou autrement. . . . Peu importe.") and *L'Idiot de la famille* ("Je l'avoue: c'est une fable. Rien ne prouve qu'il en fut ainsi. . . . N'importe.") and Sartre has remained fairly faithful to Roquentin's program. In a sense, *L'Idiot de la famille* is the novel about the writer that Roquentin also thought of writing. Literary criticism for Sartre has been inseparable from (to some degree fictionalized) biography. The self finds definition in opposition to the other. Sartre's critical production has centered on the question, Why does one choose to write?—how does someone conditioned to be a thief or a lawyer make himself into a writer?—and its basic postulate is that the creative act is not fully subject to discursive analysis and can only be recaptured imaginatively.

Critical "fictions" are, of course, inevitable. "Lying," "cheating," rearranging, are implicit in all but exact reproduction of a work, which is its own best account. I run the risk, then, of belaboring a self-destructive topic; it might be difficult to prove in rigorous fashion that Sartre's work on various writers is different from other criticism or other forms of discourse. The apparently clear distinction between "criticism" and "fiction" could easily be obnubilated. But on a simpler and more immediate level, it is unquestionable that Sartre's criticism has always contained an element of fiction or myth that separates it—at least in its intention—from forms of criticism less evidently imaginative and idiosyncratic. Sartre has never accepted the idea that each reader creates a totally new meaning from the fictional material before him. Literature is, of course, a dialectical process for Sartre, which means in part that it relies on the reader's "generous" recreation of the author's meaning. The literary object is incomplete, dependent for fullness on the reader's contribution. Nonetheless, the imaginary object remains outside the reader, not contained within his consciousness. When Sartre reads Blanchot, he claims to discover Blanchot in Blanchot, and not Sartre in Blanchot. If we believe him, then the distortion practiced in Sartre's criticism appears not to inhere so much in the occasional difficulty of recognizing the literary text through his recreation (somehow Flaubert's writings never seem themselves as I know them) but in his determined effort to use the text, to make of criticism something that goes beyond the subject matter of analysis. Sartre's critical writings have presented themselves as fictional messages, as injunctions, to his contemporaries, and they have been understood that way. Through what he lately has called "breaches of faith" (emotional weighting of vocabulary, etc.), Sartre has always more or less clearly indicated how his texts should be read. The function of his criticism, beyond its nominal task of comprehension, has been to accuse and to exhort, fundamentally, to change; it has seen itself as a fresh wind sweeping over the literary horizon, changing our perspective on everything it touches.

My project, then, is to look at Sartre's criticism with an eye to its fictional elements, to make evident imaginative imagery, emotional weighting of argument and language, and tendentious tones that crystallize provisionally into structures and, as a whole, into a morally and aesthetically oriented system. I shall consider Sartre's major works of literary criticism chronologically in order to observe the emergence of his mythology. My concerns here will be the formulation of that mythology into literary dogma, its development within an implicit ethical system, its elaboration

and modification in studies of authors politically sympathetic but essentially alien to him, and, finally, its apparent
disappearance, or hidden assumption, in his latest work.

Sartre was born in 1905. He has recently turned 70 and
appears to be reaching the end of a long career of unparal-
leled involvement in his epoch. To point out in detail that
Sartre is a man of his century would be to belabor the obvious, since over the last forty years he has absorbed and
contributed as much as any man to the intellectual makeup
of the Western world. The major writings I shall consider
were published between 1935 and 1975, between Sartre's
thirtieth and seventieth years. They simultaneously con-
tribute toward producing and are products of a climate of
opinion and currents of thought that mirror the Second
World War, the rule of Stalin, the atom bomb, Algeria, and
Vietnam—not to mention the vogue of existentialism. From
the theories of existentialism and of "committed" literature in the 1940s, through the concern expressed in 1952
in *Saint Genet* with the psychological and sociological implications of homosexuality and criminality, to the last
two decades, in which he has turned to Marxism and a
more direct political involvement, Sartre's itinerary is as
much representative as it is original.

The context of his thought spans the broadest experiences of the twentieth century, those easily familiar to
most of us and those we have read about. It includes both
Fidel Castro and Charlie Chaplin, German phenomenology
and Parisian surrealism, the Spanish Civil War and contemporary structuralism. To limit the sources and the resonances of his thought to any part of this experience seems
more than hazardous. Moreover, there have been many ex-
cellent attempts to place Sartre within the general context
of the twentieth century and it would be fruitless to repeat

much of what has already been said of him.[10] Although, in Paris at least, Sartre is no longer looked to as the innovator he once was, he remains a much discussed and important figure, and what he has represented is hardly forgotten.

The function of this study, therefore, will be to read Sartre on his own terms and to discuss his critical writing within the framework of its own vocabulary, as an independent object. The method of procedure will be implicitly Sartrian (early Sartre, perhaps), in that without seeking an explanatory structure beneath the text, I will offer a reading—a "profile," in phenomenological terms—on the level of the text itself. This will mean analyzing the more than 5000 pages of his critical works—far less known in this country than his plays and novels—closely enough to demonstrate that certain patterns of thought really do find recurrent expression there, and to convey a sense of what that criticism, at base, is about. To some degree, such a procedure, and the paraphrasing it necessarily engenders, might seem to entail a suspension of critical distance from the works treated. However, I feel no great need to defend myself against such an appearance. In discussing Sartre's views on other writers, the immediate temptation is to do to Sartre what he has done so often: attack the man and his work, accuse him of inauthenticity as he has accused others. Even assuming that one could make objective judgments about the meaning of the life of another, or that Sartre could be proved consistently inaccurate in his understanding of another writer's work, such an approach would

10. Those interested in details of Sartre's life might read Philip Thody's *Sartre: A Biographical Introduction* (London: Studio Vista, 1971). Joseph McMahon's *Humans Being: The World of Jean-Paul Sartre* (Chicago: University of Chicago Press, 1971) is among the latest of the general considerations of Sartre, and it does a good job of placing Sartre's criticism within the larger context of his life and work. See also Hazel Barnes's *Sartre* (Philadelphia: Lippincott, 1973).

seem to me self-defeating and of limited value. Baudelaire, Mallarmé, Genet, and Flaubert do not need to be defended against Sartre now. Of course he is "wrong" about them, and others; of course his judgments, more often than not, have little "scientific" or consensual validity; and one feels constrained to call attention to the most glaringly obvious distortions of his work. In fact, to speak of his criticism as a series of fictions, to say that it is formulated on the basis of a network of personal myth and not on an irreducible intellectual structure of clearly defined terms, is to take the position that on an objective basis his judgments cannot be considered "correct." But that is not the issue; the great value of Sartre's work lies not in its demonstrable accuracy or inaccuracy but in its creative genius and force, and in what it tells us about imaginative writing through Sartre's own fictional processes. The novelistic and detective story forms of *Saint Genet* and *L'Idiot de la famille,* aberrant or not, provide some of the richest and most provocative criticism of our time.[11]

One point of context must be made, however. Sartre is known primarily as an existentialist philosopher whose thought derives from Edmund Husserl and Martin Heidegger. But to an equal extent the poles of his intellectual horizon are two other masters, Freud and Marx.[12] One of

11. The focus of this study is on the fictional *content* of Sartre's criticism, but it is equally clear that Sartre frequently uses the rhetorical techniques of fiction as well. *Saint Genet*'s use of the present tense, its chapter-by-chapter suspense, *L'Idiot*'s point-by-point unravelling of a mystery, are only part of the devices of narrative that Sartre employs in the name of analysis.

12. Since the completion of this manuscript, my attention has been called to *Genèse et critique d'une autobiographie: Les Mots de Jean-Paul Sartre* (Paris: Minard, 1973), by A. James Arnold and Jean-Pierre Piriou, which presents *Les Mots* in terms of Freud's influence and comments on Sartre's attempt to link Freud and Marx. *Les Mots de Sartre* (which also works toward the elaboration of personal myth in Sartre) has a useful chapter on Sartre and Freud, parallel to and more complete than the brief introduction to the problem found here

the central paradoxes of Sartre's thought is that a man is both what others make of him and what he makes of himself; he is both a product of exterior forces and his particular situation and a free agent who chooses himself. Jean Genet, in Sartre's analysis, chooses to be what others have made of him; each act is limited in its possibilities and yet free. The questions, Why does someone choose to become a writer? What frees a man of his conditioning to allow him to negate and to criticize his world? are thus the direct focus of the problematic relation between historical forces and individual choice, and of an uneasy conjunction of an existential philosophy of liberty with a deterministic Marxist methodology, both of which Sartre attempts to support with Freudian tools of analysis. The road between Sartre's rejection of Freudian determinism in the 1940s and his neo-Marxist position in 1960 and thereafter is the same as that between his early "voluntaristic" theory of committed literature and his recent (poststructuralist) recognition that language as a system speaks through the individual. What unifies Sartre's itinerary, as much as a commitment to human freedom and a tremendous will to synthesis, is a central concern with language, writing, writers, and the creative act.

---

at the beginning of chapter 2. I have limited very strictly my discussion of Sartre's relation to Freud and Marx, principally because of the very immensity of the issues involved.

For a further understanding of Sartre's criticism in terms of its Marxism, see Fredric Jameson, *Marxism and Form* (Princeton: Princeton University Press, 1971), pp. 206–305, and "Three Methods in Sartre's Literary Criticism," in *Modern French Criticism*, ed. John K. Simon (Chicago: University of Chicago Press, 1972), pp. 193–228.

1

Situations

Situations 1

. . . le silence, comme dit Heidegger, est le mode authen-
tique de la parole.

Situations 1

In Sartre's first critical essays of the forties the correspon-
dences between a number of varied themes already begin
to make themselves clear. Especially in the essay on Brice
Parain, "Aller et retour" (1944), and in the essay on Jules
Renard, "L'homme ligoté" (1945), the poetic network of
oppositions outlined in the essay on Husserl transfers definitely to the realm of literary criticism. In these essays, the
myth of the philosopher-artist as hero is given amplified
detail and resonance and suggests a structure for the sensitivity at the base of Sartre's aesthetics. Sartre directly
transposes here the image patterns of masculine heroism
and feminine adhesive dependency, or "viscosity," to his
more literary obsessions concerning action, language, and
silence.

Throughout the essays of *Situations 1* one finds a recurrent preoccupation with the problems of language and
silence, with the artist's perception of the insufficiencies of
language, the perception that language disintegrates the
wholeness of the artist's silent intuition. It is precisely
those writers who vainly attempt to use language to express
silence and a world that precedes words who fascinate
Sartre—Parain, Bataille, Blanchot, Camus, Ponge, Faulkner.
So, in *Situations 1:*

19

> Camus "reveals his love of silence . . . in writing
> *L'Etranger* he remains silent. His sentence does not be-
> long to the universe of discourse. . . . It is measured
> very exactly by the time of a silent intuition" (111).
>
> Ponge, "ex-martyr of language . . . . was among
> those men whose literary vocation is marked by a
> furious battle against language" (227-28).
>
> "Bataille wonders how to express silence with words.
> . . . moreover, he regrets the use of discourse. He
> hates it, and through it, all language" (136-37).
>
> Blanchot explains that "the writer must speak *in or-
> der* to say *nothing*" (194).
>
> Parain's project is to destroy language and to be si-
> lent.
>
> Faulkner's dream, hidden behind an ocean of words,
> is of silence.

Sartre's preoccupation in these early essays appears in an
understanding of the novel as a form of action and not as
language, and in an antipathy for wordiness (shades of Car-
lyle!); in other essays, it centers on attempts, particularly by
the surrealists, to destroy language and on the twentieth-
century "obsession with silence" and the "crisis of language" following World War I. The problem of language
and action weaves gradually into the paradoxes of language
and silence.

"Aller et retour" [1] concerns itself with the writings of
Brice Parain. Parain, eight years Sartre's senior, is a novelist
and a philosopher of language who had helped Sartre publish *La Nausée.* In "Aller et retour" Sartre approaches
Parain's writing in terms of biography; presenting Parain as
a peasant come to the city: "Behind his moral philosophy,
his critique of language, one spots the pick and the spade"

---

1. *Situations 1,* pp. 175-226. Page references follow in the text.

(179). Parain also represents what Sartre calls peasant "muteness." "The peasant works alone, among natural forces that don't need to be named in order to act. He keeps still" (130). Sartre has now created a new element in his mythology: the silent peasant, man alone heroically facing nature, the man of action walking his mother earth, his awaiting, feminine land. Parain, the peasant, is a man of action ("Parain deliberately refuses contemplative joys . . . he accords primacy to *practical* action over all. Man is a being who acts." [179]), springing forth from "enormous earthy silences," and a man alone. Action, silence, solitude —a pattern begins to take shape. Parain, silent peasant, leaves his land, and is faced, at the *Ecole Normale,* with the glib, easy talkers of the city, with Sartre himself. He comes to the city, meets the talkers, and learns "intellectual gymnastics," the weightless brilliance of polemics, the games of intellection, rhetoric, and language. To join society he must make this language his; like Jean Cayrol's peasant Gaspard in *Les Corps Etrangers,* he must use the language of others, wear the language of the bourgeoisie like a foreign body. To join society he must cease to act and begin to talk; he must sacrifice authentic nature to theatrics. To the peasant, separated from his land, no longer alone, language is from the first a betrayal.

Parain sees this betrayal as a betrayal of intuition. "He will always see words through a thickness of muteness. . . . In 1922, he calls this silence *instinct* and opposes it to speech which is 'eloquence' or 'polemics.' When things are understood, one remains silent. The lamp is on the table, everyone works, while sensing the mute presence of the others: there is an order of silence" (182).[2] According

2. There is a fascinating reversal of this tableau in Simone de Beauvoir's *Tout Compte fait* (Paris: Gallimard, 1972), p. 107, in the description by Sartre's mother of a scene from Sartre's childhood. Near the end of her life,

to Sartre, Parain is haunted by the idea of intuitive, immediate knowledge, which was also the impulse behind surrealism. He remains always in search of silence, or really of
what Sartre refers to as "infrasilence," that silence prior to
language which one might postulate as coincident with
some state of nature. He reaches for a lost paradise of
man's unity with nature, where the word did not interpose
itself between intuition and the object, between man and
his desire, between man and his need. In "Un nouveau
mystique," [3] the essay on Parain's contemporary, Georges
Bataille, Sartre saw that Bataille shared the same vision of
language destroying man's unity. "To speak is to tear oneself apart, to put off existing until later, until the end of
the act of speaking, to split oneself between a subject, a
verb, a predicate. M. Bataille wants to exist totally and immediately: in the very moment. . . . Silence and the moment being none other than one and the same thing . . ."
(136-37). And in 1970 Sartre is still working over the same
problem in reference to André Puig's novel, L'Inachevé: if
realism as exhaustive discourse cannot recreate the mute
intuition of total being, then how can the author render
the intuition of a totality without parts through language,
which is discursive in its very nature? [4]

It would be a sad mistake to equate Sartre's complex
musings about the nature of the universe with Parain's up-
dated romanticism (as Sartre depicts it), or to attribute
Parain's interests directly to Sartre. In fact, elsewhere in

Sartre's mother started to write a correction of *Les Mots,* feeling that her son
had totally misunderstood his childhood. Yet she had to admit that she had
learned something from her son, that all was not quite well at their home: "I
see us again in the evening, under the lamp, my parents, my brothers, and me.
But I realize that in fact we didn't talk to each other. Everyone was all alone."
  3. *Situations 1,* pp. 133-74.
  4. *Situations 9* (Paris: Gallimard, 1972), p. 283.

his writings Sartre destroys at length both the myth of primitive man alone with nature and the "myth" of the metaphysical problem of language; in "Aller et retour" he finds Parain in Parain's writings, and not Sartre. Simone de Beauvoir quotes a letter from Sartre, who says that while Parain is an intelligent man, he spends his time on problems that do not have any real interest, among them language and the inexhaustible depth of words.[5] She also tells us that Sartre's interest is not in language, but in "communication." At the end of the essay on Parain, Sartre outlines a critique of Parain's ideas, to the effect that the metaphysical problem of language does not exist. "Language is nothing other than existence in the presence of the other . . . it is that mute and desperate dialogue. Language is being-for-others . . . if it is true that to speak means to act under the gaze of the other, the celebrated problems of language run the grave risk of being nothing but a regional specification of the great problem of the existence of the other" (219-20). The problem is the relationship between men, and language becomes problematic only as a mode of that relationship.

Furthermore, Sartre will come to believe that man is never alone and has never been alone. In his "Prière pour le bon usage de Genet" in *Saint Genet* he writes, "For a long time we believed in the social atomism bequeathed to us by the eighteenth century, and it seemed to us that man was by nature a solitary entity who entered into relations with his fellow men *afterward*. Thus, solitude appeared to be our original state; one emerged from it if all went well, but one could return to it if one's luck changed. We now know that this is nonsense. The truth is that 'human reality' 'is-in-society' as it 'is-in-the-world'; it is neither a nature nor a state; it is made" (634).

5. *La Force de l'âge* (Paris: Gallimard, 1960), p. 307.

We must recognize, then, that our tentative construct of
Sartre's imagination will often be contradicted by developments in Sartre's discursive thought. What we are aiming at
here are hypothesized, unexamined, and autonomous
reservoirs of imagination that might precede prosaic, logical
delineation but that are nonetheless present in the text.
Parain's mythic vision of the peasant matches a cluster of
corresponding images in Sartre's imagination at a time
when Sartre had apparently not yet discovered the fallacies
of social atomism; despite his nascent reservations he can
still say that he generally accepts most of Parain's analyses.
He contests only the conclusions to which they lead. He
can accept Parain's analysis because it rhymes with his own
early intuition, perhaps because Jean-Paul once played at
being the hero of a silent movie, perhaps because it echoes
clearly the vision of man outlined in one of Sartre's early
texts entitled "La Légende de la vérité."[6]

Sartre wrote "La Légende de la vérité" in 1929, at the
age of 24; a fragment of it was published in 1931. In this
tale in the form of a Platonic myth, Sartre depicted the
creation of "truth" as a product of commerce. Before the
creation of truth, before the existence of a "marketplace
for words," was a world of wandering nomads and workers,
at one with nature, alone with themselves, heedless of the
possibility of a unique model for truth. With the invention
of truth, man was no longer "alone with himself" and this
primitive world gave way to the cheating, squalid circus of
the ideologists. In these nomads, these "thaumaturges who,
excluded from the city, from its logic and calculus, wander
alone in the desert," [7] as Simone de Beauvoir speaks of

6. In Michel Contat and Michel Rybalka, *Les Ecrits de Sartre* (Paris: Gallimard, 1970), pp. 531–46. The heroic peasant is present elsewhere in Sartre's
writings—for instance, in Brunet, of *Les Chemins de la liberté,* who has peasant
hands, despite his intellectual nature.

7. *La Force de l'âge*, p. 50.

them, we can see the model for the silent peasant of "Aller et retour" and the sources of Sartre's sympathy for him. If in "Aller et retour" the peasant works alone and is silent, then in "La Légende de la vérité" he is equally alone with nature, and "Nature says neither yes nor no . . . it is still";[8] if Parain thinks he has betrayed original unity by speaking, then so has the nomad been betrayed and divided from himself and his thoughts. "For a long time, man had produced his thoughts like his life, they adhered to his body . . . they had no other tie with things than the great universal sympathy," [9] but universal sympathy no longer exists, and man's thoughts no longer cleave to his body.

The discontinuous perceptions we see at the back of Sartre's mind in these early writings develop into a first form of cohesion in the essay on Jules Renard, a turn-of-the-century writer from the same isolated region of France that Genet was raised in, Le Morvan, who is best known for his *Journal* and for *Poil de carotte*. In "L'homme ligoté," [10] which directly evolves from the preoccupations of the essays on Parain and Ponge, certain strands of Sartre's approach to literature come together for the first time, and Sartre's intuitions translate themselves into literary theory. Sartre seems almost to have chosen Renard to bring together the ends of the question: first because, according to Sartre, Renard "created the literature of silence" (271); secondly, because, in contrast to his fascination with Parain and Ponge, Sartre dislikes Renard.

Creator of the "literature of silence," Renard is precisely the man who has betrayed his peasant heritage. He has left behind him generations of muteness, the "virile" silence of short peasant sentences bred deeply into him by the forces

8. Contat and Rybalka, *Les Ecrits de Sartre*, p. 544. My translations.
9. Ibid., p. 534.
10. *Situations 1*, pp. 271–89.

of nature, to come to the salons of the city to talk and to write. "There was something gnarled and solitary about Renard . . . a genuine villager's misanthropy. . . . But this taciturn man had a taste for writing; he came to Paris to play 'the original,' he sought out company to show off his solitude . . . he came to be silent through writing. He wanted to shine . . . finally, this taste for muteness brings him back to chatter. . . . Renard's *Journal* is laconic chatter [*bavardage*], his entire work pointillism" (272, 275). Renard has left behind him silence, solitude, action, and manliness; and like Parain, like Genet, like Jean-Paul in *Les Mots,* he does it to be liked, to seduce, to have friends, and to join society—to communicate, superficially, though not to "commune."

With this traitor Sartre makes an indirect yet startlingly obvious self-identification through common father figures: "His father was one of those village originals, as was also my paternal grandfather, who, disappointed in his marriage contract, didn't address three words to my grandmother in forty-five years, and whom she called 'my pensionary' " (271). This identification is supported in tone and signification throughout the essays, in which Sartre makes further identifications of himself as a traitor. In an essay on a novel by André Gorz,[11] he demonstrates that both he and Gorz are necessarily traitors because they are intellectuals; at the end of *Les Mots* he says of himself, "I became a traitor and have remained one" (238); in *Plaidoyer pour les intellectuels* the writer is shown to be an intellectual in his essence, and the intellectual a traitor and a "monster." What Sartre sees in Renard is both a recognition and a rejection of self: the self-rejection and self-accusation of being a *bavard de salon,* a glib *normalien* as seen by the

11. "Des rats et des hommes," in *Situations 4* (Paris: Gallimard, 1964), pp. 38-84.

peasant Parain, and a traitor. He sees himself as having betrayed the paternal heritage of silence, tricked by a false Moses who replaced the true father, "child of silence."

In order to rediscover that heritage, like Perceval or Stephen Dedalus, he would have to leave his mother behind, which would constitute a second betrayal. Certainly one of the most striking parts of Sartre's autobiography is the pathetic passage that concludes the first part of *Les Mots*, the scene that ends Sartre's age of innocence. At the age of eight, having lived "without brother or sister or friends," Jean-Paul discovers "my true judges, my contemporaries, my peers, and their indifference condemned me. I could not get over discovering myself through them: neither a wonder nor a jellyfish. Just a little shrimp in whom no one was interested. . . . [My mother] would take my hand, we would go from tree to tree and from group to group, always entreating, always excluded" (134–35). At this point he fails to enter society: "Until the age of ten, I remained alone between an old man and two women" (83). Although at times his mother is a sister to him, although at times their union is so close that they are together but one young girl ("through her I learned to scent the male, to fear him, to hate him" [219]), she remains nevertheless a "stranger" for him, as his father was a stranger for her; even in this sort of union he remains alone in a world separated from the others, living apart from his audience, across the footlights in a "proud exile that quickly turned to anguish" (84).

When he breaks from this solitude, Sartre is caught up in a complex social round of betrayal and seduction. The paternal heritage has been stolen from him, he has turned against it; he has been abducted to a feminine, motherly world, a theatre where his role is to play the coquette, the seducer, grandfather's charming little girl, and where he remains alone. This world must be abandoned; the falsely comforting, uneasy, provisional unity of mother and son is broken by the presence of the Other. Jean-Paul goes off to school, but at first he finds in his schoolmates merely a new audience to please. In a sense, this little drama epitomizes the dilemma of the writer as Sartre understands it in his early criticism: until he has found his full authenticity, the writer inevitably begins by betraying himself and the unity of his solitary silent intuition at the very moment he uses language, the moment he attempts to communicate. Communication is a form of seduction, and language can serve as the tool of that seduction. At this moment, Sartre understands language as analytic and bourgeois,[12] as a betrayal of sympathetic comprehension and human communion, despite the fact that in part it defines both. The writer may be to some degree a hero, but, to the same degree, he is a traitor.

Sartre as phenomenologist, as novelist, as essayist, is he who describes, who writes, who talks, who seduces. The need for self-justification and the justification itself are immediate; one has only to understand that language as a tool must approach action, that talking must never be useless, and that "intellectual gymnastics" can never be only a game, but must aim instead at being an act. Seduction must change from an end in itself to a means to justified ends. The writer must recover his betrayed masculinity by changing mincing bavardage into heroism, futile words into acts, language into action, language into silence, and social atomism into unity. Renard "spent his childhood in the midst of peasants, who, each in his own way, proclaimed the uselessness of speech" (271), and Sartre has got their message. He must find a way to use words. A first definition of the problematic nature of literature, a style, and an

12. In *Saint Genet* he will first recognize its synthetic aspects.

eventual yet remarkably clear link to Marxism are born here. "The quest for truth," Sartre will say in *Qu'est-ce que la littérature?*, "takes place in and by language conceived as a certain kind of instrument."[13]

What must be shown is the centrality of this choice in Sartre's criticism and the directions he moves in from this basis. He makes the first connecting steps in "L'homme ligoté." In the considerations of the opposition of peasant silence and Parisian bavardage there first emerges what must be considered an essential Sartrian literary principle and criterion of judgment: "On peut bavarder en cinq mots comme en cinq lignes. Il suffit de préférer la phrase aux idées" (One can chatter in five words as well as in five lines. All that is needed is to prefer the expression to the ideas) (275).

In his early criticism Sartre very definitely contrasts thought and language. Somehow, thought appears to be more meaty and substantial than its ordinary expression, and, as a consequence, the proper use of language is to aim at a philosophical precision and density, an effectiveness and directness, that embody the weightiness of its message. Renard's mistake is to confuse the gravid silence of comprehension and thought with briefness in speech. "All his life he believed that style was the art of making things short. And without a doubt it is true that the most concise form of expression is ordinarily the best. However, this means: concise in relation to the ideas expressed. Thus certain long sentences by Descartes or by Proust are very short, because what they say could not be said in fewer words" (273).

13. *What Is Literature?*, trans. Bernard Frechtman (New York: Washington Square Press, 1966), p. 4. Page references will be to this edition (with some changes in the translation) and will follow in the text. Originally published as "Qu-est-ce que la littérature?" in *Situations 2* (Paris: Gallimard, 1948).

There are a number of points to be drawn from this passage. First of all, in the remark that *ordinarily* the most concise form of expression is the best, Sartre codifies a whole gamut of his tastes. In the light of this idea one can understand, for example, his dislike in *Situations 1* of Faulkner's "volubility," and his description of Faulknerian conversation as pasty and flaccid. For Sartre's taste, Faulkner's style is too abstract, preachy, superb, too poetic and pseudo-magical; in sum, too long. He calls Faulkner a "lyric novelist," "a teller of tales, a liar" (11), half-sincere, half-dreamer, he keeps secrets, he tells *just a little* in half-phrases he hopes will pass unnoticed. He is, in Sartre's eyes, an artist and, at the same time, almost the equivalent of a cheap magician, an "illusionist," dishonest and disloyal, hiding, behind a stream of verbosity, an impossible world, which he tricks the reader into accepting.

Consistent in *Situations 1* is an attack on romantic inspiration expressed as long-windedness. Sartre opposes the unchecked romantic flow of words and the rush of oratorical movements to the concision of classical restraint. The classical ideal is economy, the expression of an idea in the clearest minimal form; and the classical style has a practical effect on the world, whereas the romantic style is only verbal.[14] It is in these terms that Sartre expresses his admiration for Camus: "The turn of his reasoning, the clarity of his ideas, the cut of his essayist's style . . . everything proclaims him a classicist" (94). Meursault is an example for Sartre of a "virile silence," a refusal to indulge in orgies of words; *L'Etranger,* "that clear, dry work" (112), is born of a struggle within Camus against a tendency toward poetic prose, and the result is a triumph of authentic expression that creates "a brusque communion of two men, the author and the reader" (99). At this stage in Sartre's

14. Cf. *L'Idiot de la famille* (Paris: Gallimard, 1971), p. 1374.

thought, for a brief moment, the true prose artist appears
to be an icy yet impassioned (hence, nonmechanistic) ana-
lyst, whose tools are precision, humor (used as a weapon),
and a "scientist's eye," and in whose writing exist elements
of sudden violence, of brusque and dry hardness. His function is to cut critically into the world of men—not to observe it passively as a "realist" would, but to slice it to
pieces and to lay it out uncovered.

Contained within the comparison of romantic-verbal and
classical-practical styles there lies an unresolved argument
about artistic abandon and artistic distance, about the artist
as a trickster-manipulator and as participant, as *témoin*
("witness") and as *complice* ("accomplice"). Central to
this discussion is, of course, the famous essay "M. François
Mauriac et la liberté."[15] Sartre denounces in it the "treachery" inherent in Mauriac's novels and the treachery Mauriac
demands of the reader by writing of his characters at once
from an interior viewpoint, as their complice, and from an
external, distant, omnisciently Godlike viewpoint, as their
judge, their témoin. "The novelist may be [the characters']
witness or their accomplice, but never both at once. In or
out" (44). Like Faulkner, Mauriac plays tricks; he has
robbed his characters of their (novelistic) liberty; what is
more, he has defined the limits of Sartre's admiration for
classicism in the novel. In playing God-as-critical-artist,
Mauriac is led to emblematic scene staging, to a theatrical
form of concision that is only dramatic eloquence and illusory ceremony. He has gone beyond the bounds of Sartre's
taste, beyond what Sartre will allow the novelist at this
point. "*La Fin de la Nuit* is not a novel. Could you label
'novel' this angulous, glacial work with its theatrical passages, its bits of analysis, its poetic meditations? These
jerky starts and violent applications of the brakes, these

15. *Situations 1*, pp. 33-52.

painful resumptions and breakdowns, can you confuse
them with the majestic course of novelistic time? Will you
let yourself be taken in by this immobile narrative, which
betrays at first glance its intellectual armature, in which
the mute figures of the heroes are inscribed like angles in a
circle?" (51). Mauriac has perverted the practical ideal of
classicism and destroyed the novel, which Sartre understands as majestic breadth and density, movement and
action.

Mauriac is guilty in Sartre's eyes of the grossest and most
evident artifice. What might weaken Sartre's attack on
Mauriac is that in Sartre's eyes all art is artifice: it cheats,
it "lives by appearances." The act of writing itself puts the
artist in a false position. Whether analytic or poetic, judg-
ing or sympathetic, concise or bombastic in style, the artist's work is imbued a priori with illusionism; it begins as
betrayal. All the same, this argument in no way helps
Mauriac, for even in this framework there do exist for
Sartre preferred choices that can be made within certain
limits. He distinguishes here, for example—and he will develop and to some extent negate this idea in *Qu'est-ce que
la littérature?*—between tricking the reader by a technique
in which intention and process are clear (as in Dos Passos,
where artificial techniques appear semilegitimate to Sartre
because they are reversible and are evident to the reader
who can judge them in their artificiality and beauty) and
tricking the reader by the continuous, insidious onslaught
of style: "There are two kinds of pictures: real pictures
and the illusionist kind" (7). Style as the essence of con-
ventional literary procedure Sartre understands as indirect,
hidden, and manipulatory, to a degree that robs the reader
of his freedom and his creativity. Style, properly understood, should only be a technique subservient to a message,
and separable from that message; after all, Sartre would

claim, it is not an act, but only a *geste* ("gesture," "posture").

Within the ordinary limits of literary artifice the most concise expression is the best. The wrapping on the package should be kept to a minimum. But Renard goes beyond the point to which Sartre is willing to apply this idea. While the economy of Ponge's style pleases Sartre and makes his poems seem like "bevelled constructions, with each facet a paragraph" (249), in which each sentence has density, definition, internal cohesion, and constitutes in itself a "minutely articulated world, in which the place of each word has been calculated" (255), the excessive economy of Renard's sentences causes them to resemble those "solid, rudimentary animals, for whom a single hole serves as mouth and meatus" (273). Still, in reference to Proust and Descartes, Sartre stipulates that the length of a sentence is only consequent to the weightiness of the thought. Certain writers are to be permitted lengthy expression and extraordinary complexity of development. How are we to know them?

Renard's main default is that he is guilty of bavardage, of literary chatter (Heidegger's "Gerede," which Sartre translates as "parlerie"). In *Situations 1,* Nabokov sins in the same way: he is too literary, he has read too much; like his heroes, he is too self-aware, too critical; he is a bavard, masochistic and gratuitous. In other words, he is a stylist, he prefers words to thoughts.[16] To transcend this ordinary condition of the writer, it is only necessary to reverse the

16. In the same way, Sartre accuses Camus, in their famous argument, of having written a letter "trop écrite." Implicit in both accusations is a repeat of the attack on intellectuals and stylists as traitors: "Intelligence stinks" (*Situations 4*, p. 64). The problem can be traced through to *Plaidoyer pour les intellectuels,* where Sartre gives a different view; the role of the intellectual in Sartre's earlier writings has been discussed by Victor Brombert in *The Intellectual Hero* (Philadelphia: Lippincott, 1961), pp. 219–49.

terms of the equation, to prefer the thought to the expression, the matter to the form.

"It may seem surprising that Renard had nothing to say. . . . For lack of having chosen a new way to see, he looks everywhere vainly for new things to see" (276-77). In contrast to Renard, the true Sartrian artist has something to say,[17] he has a new way of seeing, and his only struggle is to put that silent intuition into words. He must express his understanding of the human condition in a way that will create a bond of communion with other men; he must change the world. "In effect, it is a matter of penetrating the real" (282). Unlike Renard, he cannot be passive, he cannot timidly observe and contemplate, he cannot docilely accept the given, but he must contest it, he must act, and his thought must become action, directed toward a specific goal through language. His writing must act in a real fashion upon reality, within a specific situation—he must refuse a dissatisfaction with everything because that accomplishes nothing concrete. He must, like Dos Passos, create a desire for revolution in his readers; he must make the reader ashamed and guilty and change his world.

Renard is not capable of this action and has nothing to say because, Sartre implies, he is a coward, or, to be more exact, an effeminate coward and a formalist. He escapes out of reality into a verbal world of *cocasserie* ("drollery") and *gentillesse* ("gracefulness") (284), into an elitist, autistic, comfortable, protected world of positivism and art. At one moment he has sensed an intuitive world of silence and action, but backed timorously away from it:

It would have been necessary to lose control, to approach the object alone. But Renard never loses con-

17. In *Plaidoyer* the something that the writer has to say is given quite a different meaning, but in *L'Idiot* it seems to correspond more directly to this simple formulation.

trol. . . . He kept quiet, he did nothing . . . stuffed, muzzled . . . sterilized . . . he found no resources but dreams. His images, which at first were supposed to dig into reality like claws, quickly became instant reveries, at the margin of things. He was too afraid of leaving his feet to dream of building beyond this world a universe that would have been his own. He quickly returned to things, to his friends, to his decoration, and the dreams that were the most persistent—because they were the least dangerous—limited themselves to stroking the image of a nice, dull little adultery that he rarely dared commit. In the same way, his *Journal,* which started off as an exercise in severe lucidity, becomes very quickly a shadowy and tepid corner of shameful complicity with himself. [288]

Afraid of solitude, Renard hides in the crowds of literary Paris, in the ranks of the realists; afraid of true communion in society, he is only his own complice. Afraid of silence, he is a bavard; afraid of language as a total human enterprise, he mutilates language and says nothing. Afraid of action, he takes flight from reality into onanistic dreams and into a formal conception of beauty as decoration and voluptuousness.

In response to Renard, Sartre adds another axiom to his critical framework, "Quant à la beauté, elle vient par surcroît, quand elle peut" (As for beauty, it's thrown in to boot, where possible) (286). Language and style must take a second place to thought; beauty must take a second place to action. Beauty is not the essence of literature, but may be present there, hidden in accidental resonances and supplemental suggestions, lurking in the bushes as poetry, a magical "captation" or appropriation of the world. The novel appears to hold a privileged position for Sartre because for him it must embody the majestic materiality of thought, the brusqueness and dryness of action; in it beauty and style are secondary formal considerations and are suspect to a great degree.

Sartre's Renard, girdled, "ligoté" in his style, traitor, bavard de salon, is an emblem of bad and inauthentic writing. What he should be, and is not, is "prophète," "maudit," or "combattant." He should commit himself to presenting a total picture of mankind that would change and deepen the human condition. In *Situations 1,* there seem to be two such writers, beyond Husserl, Dos Passos, and Camus. The first is Francis Ponge, contemporary poet and author of *Le Parti pris des choses.* Of all the essays of *Situations 1,* it is the essay on Ponge, "L'homme et les choses," [18] along with the article on Husserl, that bear the greatest interest for contemporary theoreticians. The famous attack on Mauriac, with its plea for existentially free protagonists, can no longer be taken to offer acceptable critical concepts, and the Dos Passos essay, in retrospect, is almost embarrassing in its exaggerated claims. Sartre's work on Blanchot and Faulkner, on the other hand, remains of great value, and its insights have been absorbed into modern criticism. But the Ponge essay is still most problematic and vital, particularly on account of its concentration on the relationship of words and reality. More assimilable than his latest theories of language, which tread on the toes of post-Saussurean terminology,[19] Sartre's thought in "L'homme et les choses" is close enough to contemporary discussions of language—while also just different enough—to make it interesting.

18. *Situations 1*, pp. 226–70. For further discussion of this essay, see Steven Ungar, "Sartre, Ponge and the Ghost of Husserl," *Sub-stance* 8 (Winter, 1974): 139–50.

19. See, for example, Christine Glucksman in a valuable article in "L'Origine de la littérature" in *L'Arc* 30 (1966): 53–59.

What Sartre discerns in Ponge's use of language is the creation of an independent, self-sufficient, and self-referential
system of signifiers that do not docilely transpose the
phenomena to which they ostensibly refer into linguistic
experience but instead become self-revealing objects in
themselves. According to Sartre, Ponge, having assimilated
a world of objects, discovers that world living an autonomous life within him as language, and nature outside him
begins to exist as petrified language. At first, like Parain,
like the surrealists, he attempts to negate those worlds, to
destroy words with other words, only to find himself still
speaking a human language. What he then discovers are the
turgid lumps and swellings of words, their secret, personal,
adventitious and useless meanings, born of their history
and the clumsiness of their users (232). The discovery
leads him to try to strip words of their socialized significations, to seize them at the moment they are about to become independent objects. For Roquentin in the tramway
or before the chestnut tree in the public garden, things lose
their labels and human names. So does Ponge separate the
signifying object from its a priori anthropocentric context.
Through doubt, Husserlian naiveté, and love, he takes on
the role of the phenomenological hero in search of things
themselves. He seeks to purify words, to go beyond the
negative surrealist moment to a constructive "revolution of
language" (234). The economy of his laconic style is active
and affirmative, as, for instance, Renard's style is not; he
names anew.

Or rather, Sartre concludes, that is his goal. Ponge never
quite becomes the Sartrian hero he might have been. Unlike Genet, he never goes far enough, because he does not
doubt everything. He never gets around to a methodical
doubting of science, and his vision, which might have been
pure, falls back at important instances on his scientific

knowledge and on an underlying mechanistic preconcep-
tion of the universe. He cheats, in other words; he does not
keep faith. In this light, Sartre sees Ponge's revolutionary
enterprise as an example of bad faith. It becomes for him a
"necrological dream" of an "inoffensive and radical catas-
trophe" (265): the burying of mankind beneath matter,
the mineralization of the human. Ponge's attempt to
change the world reveals itself to Sartre as ultimately petu-
lant, like that of Flaubert in some ways, and as futile,
merely personal and self-inflating, contemptuous of man.
It does not have to be taken seriously because in the end
Sartre can reduce it to metaphor.

But where Ponge fails as a model for the writer, Paul
Nizan does not. Nizan was a Marxist novelist who had been
Sartre's schoolboy friend, and Sartre offers Nizan to us,
not just as a model of literary intention and procedure, but
also as a model of style. "One enjoys rediscovering . . .
Nizan's bitter, somber personality . . . and his handsome,
dry, negligent style, his long Cartesian sentences, which
drop off in the middle, as if they couldn't hold themselves
up any longer, and suddenly leap up to finish in the
heights; and those orator's transports that suddenly cut
short and give way to a curt, icy maxim: not the style of a
novelist, cunning and indirect: a style of struggle, a
weapon [*un style de combat, une arme*]" (28).[20]

What Sartre admires in his friend (who "retained, through

20. At this stage, literature seems suspect for Sartre in its essence because it
is indirect, because it does not rely on documentary solidity and clarity. In
this respect, the distance from *Situations 1* to *Plaidoyer*, where Sartre sees the
value of literature to lie in its essential ambivalence (see chapter 4), is immense. Francis Jeanson, in his *Sartre par lui-même* (Paris: Editions de Seuil,
1969), puts all of Sartre's work in this light as desire to seduce and convince
and as desire to appeal to the liberty of the reader. In Sartre's description of
Nizan here, it is particularly important that the "novelist's" style is rejected;
Sartre wants something more forceful and brusque.

fidelity to his childhood, a kind of rustic naturalism,") he explains most clearly in *Situations 4* in his preface to the 1960 edition of Nizan's *Aden Arabie*[21]—Nizan "said no to the end" (126). For Sartre, Nizan was a "spoilsport," a furious "young monster, a handsome young monster" (125), who speaks across the years of hate, of unsatisfied desire, and of destruction. His revolt, intransigent, desperate, and extreme, is an "exemplary" one, as his scandalous life and tortured existence are "exemplary." His work? "It sought to displease: that's its greatest merit" (117). His writing, a tool used to a social end, is a call to arms, and so Nizan can speak to new generations of angry young men: "Who can enlighten their violence? Nizan, he's their man" (124).

"Young and full of rage, struck down by sudden death" (125), Nizan wrote prose that Sartre describes as youthful and tough. His violence is particularly telling because it is in itself a denunciation of the complacent bourgeois and of Sartre himself, and because it is a political violence. The relation between Sartre's political views and his literary judgments has always been clear—in his attacks on bourgeois society and on Baudelaire and Flaubert as bourgeois, in his embrace of the revolutionary artist—but nowhere is the coincident element of guilt and self-judgment more explicit. The bourgeois artist is only a *littérateur;* Gide and Valéry, "those two overly famous bourgeois, had a high opinion of themselves; each day they bedecked their twin souls in public and thought they were revealing themselves in their naked truth" (115). Literary commitment is here

21. Reprinted in *Situations 4,* pp. 130–88. Page references are to the translation by Benita Eisler in *Situations* (New York: Braziller, 1965). One of Nizan's exemplary acts echoes Sartre's article on Husserl: in the blazing heat of Aden, Nizan "took an open car and set off down the road, without a hat, at high noon." The hero still lives in an open world of dazzling light.

not enough; Sartre, stepson of a "polytechnician," and his
bourgeois literary fellows have betrayed their own youth
("so many times that it is only decent to ignore it in
silence" [124]); they are now old men. "We have nothing
left to say to these young men. Fifty years of living in the
backward province that France has become are degrading.
We shouted, protested, signed and countersigned. We de-
clared, according to our habits of thinking, 'It is not per-
missible . . . ,' or, 'The proletariat will not tolerate . . .'
And now at last, here we are. So we have accepted everything. . . . [Our pain] comes from our arteries; strange
objects, half eaten away by nature, covered with ants, we
look like those tepid drinks, those idiotic paintings which
amused Rimbaud" (124-25). Sartre condemns himself in
the same terms he will condemn Baudelaire. I have been,
he says, not a revolutionary, but only a *révolté*, a rebel
who wanted to keep a certain order in existence so I could
attack it; in comparison with Nizan's wild passion, I offered only "the dignity of an old wife" (148).

In the end, however, Nizan comes back to the same
problem that Sartre has always faced: words. Although
Sartre claims that Nizan was the better writer, that words
came to him more easily, and were therefore less important to him, he was nonetheless primarily a writer, and
limited by that condition. His response to the problem of
writing, as Sartre explains it, is not hard to understand; as
a Communist, he saw that language belonged to the bourgeois masters and had to be taken aggressively from them:
"A book can be an act if the revolutionary writer sets
about deconditioning language" (160). For Sartre, then,
Nizan's writing was aimed at the proper ideal for literature
and centered on the proper problem: literature must be
an act; literature is language.

Situations 2

Songes et mensonges, superstitions: poésie.

Saint Genet

All literature, Sartre says at the end of *Qu'est-ce que la littérature?* (1948), consists essentially in taking a position. Literature is a choice of perspective, a *prise de position* toward the world and toward the self, which is expressed and discovered through words. In the face of the impossibility of the human condition, it is a way out (*issue*) of the "mousetrap" of situation; it is an invention of the self, through the full, free usage of all the creative faculties.

In the search for truth, the writer's only tools are words. If, as Sartre's contemporaries claim, language suffers from a cancerous disease, then for him the writer's task is to cure it: "The function of a writer is to call a spade a spade." (196). Echoing elements of the essay on Ponge, Sartre asks of the writer that he reestablish language in its purest dignity; specifically, he must open the doors to new ideas through the control of new words and he must analytically cleanse words of their adventitious, merely formal and material senses and resonances to restore their clear and useful meanings. That is, he must strip the poetic element away from prose: "There is nothing more unfortunate [*néfaste*] than the literary practice which, I believe, is called poetic prose and which consists of using words for the obscure harmonics which resound about them and which are made up of vague meanings which are in contradiction with the clear signification" (197).[22] The *issue* that

22. Here, I believe, lie the elements of a Sartrian correction of Ponge and even of Flaubert in *L'Idiot*. By 1972 the issue is more complex, but at this early point the purity of language is not to be established by a return to a state of language before its socialization, but by insistence on its pragmatic signification.

the writer invents is total; it includes, in addition to his subjects, his style and his technique. He cannot, therefore, permit himself a childlike enjoyment of language for its own sake, because that would transform literature into a form of mystification or illusionism. Literature must be demystified, and the writer must strive to communicate clearly, without pretending to hint at the incommunicable. "Our thought is no better than our language, and it ought to be judged by the way it uses language" (197). Nor will Sartre permit the unconscious or the involuntary to be invoked as the ultimate reality of literature, for in 1948 Sartre believes that a writer *only means what he says:* if he had wanted to say something else, he would have said it.

According to Sartre, the task of literature and of criticism in the twentieth century has also become total; it demands an entire commitment. Literature must become an act, and the literature of the future will be a literature of praxis. The questions that man poses for himself are moral ones. Literature must be an aggressive answering of those questions, an ethical choosing that is both difficult and disquieting. Therefore, writing can no longer be description or explication or narration, because "description . . . is pure contemplative enjoyment; explanation is acceptance, it excuses everything. Both of them assume that the die is cast" (201). Literature is dying; it no longer has anything to do in contemporary society. The traditional uses of prose are no longer possible because they are forms of passivity; a new literature is to be invented in which perception itself will be a form of action, a revealing (*dévoilement*) of the world in the perspective of possible change.

Qu'est-ce que la littérature? itself, Sartre's best known programmatic critical text, is obviously enough a prise de position within a traditional framework: to save literature, Sartre states, it is necessary to take a position within literature. The major arguments of *Qu-est-ce que la littéra-ture?* are well known and have been frequently discussed. They concern themselves, for the most part, with the principles of "committed" literature and the social responsibility of the writer; they lead to the conclusions above and to an almost journalistic conception of literature as ideologically concerned with present-day problems, as a dialectical exercise in creative "generosity" on the part of both reader and writer, as negativity and construction, as an appeal for practical change and freedom, as a revelation of injustices, and finally as representing an integrating and militant function within society. This essay, with the other articles assembled in *Situations 2* ("Présentation des Temps modernes" and "La Nationalisation de la littérature"), establishes for Sartre a rounded critical position, setting for the next twenty-five years the major lines of his views of the relations of literature to language, society, and the individual. (His work in *L'Imaginaire* completes his position; from this stage to the reworked viewpoint in the late sixties of *Plaidoyer pour les intellectuels* and "L'Ecrivain et sa langue," the developments in Sartre's theory can be measured most clearly. These last two texts will be discussed in the final chapter.) We can see the genesis of this elaborated position in the obsessions of *Situations 1,* which find expression in *Situations 2* in an attack on cowardice in literature.

First, there is in *Qu'est-ce que la littérature?* an attack on "pure" literature, an indictment of the "grave error of pure stylists" (13), based on the investigations in *Situations 1* into language. The error of the stylists (which Sartre speaks of elsewhere as the incredible stupidity of "des forts en thème"), the mistake of those who prefer expression to thought, is to believe that words are winds blowing over the surface of things, touching them without changing them. Sartre proclaims, with many of his contemporaries, that to speak is to act, and that to name something is to change it. Words, speech, are "a certain particular moment of action" that has no meaning except as a prolongation of the senses and physical action. To write is to speak; the writer, by which Sartre really means *prosateur,* "is a *speaker;* he designates, demonstrates, orders, refuses, challenges, begs, insults, persuades, insinuates" (11). That is to say, the writer is a certain kind of man of action, and writing is an act, an uncertain, solitary enterprise that involves risk and danger and demands courage.

At question here, of course, is Sartre's notoriously arbitrary distinction between the poet and the writer, between the poetic attitude and the attitude of the prose writer. Sartre's poet is a man who refuses to *use* words, who takes them as objects rather than signs. So, he is not a "speaker," he does not name and change the world; poets "do not speak, neither do they keep still; it is something different" (15). Poetry assumes man's defeat; it is a commitment to failure, based particularly on a vision of the inadequacies of language to express everything, which makes of failure a final value, a contestation and appropriation of the universe. It is the mythic humanism of "loser wins," which ignores the practical uses of things, and so, unlike prose, it does not have to be an act. The essence of prose, on the other hand, the impulse behind communication, Sartre sees as the aspiration to success (though not necessarily its achievement—see p. 81 below).

Implicit here, too, are problems arising from the notion of style. The stylists' error is based on the idea of a "value" carried in each text, separable from its content, and to be found intuitively in the involuntary resonances of beauty and style. For Sartre, at this point, a text is not to be handled only intuitively, since "intuition is silence, and the end of language is to communicate" (13). A written work is based on the decision to communicate to others certain ideas, results obtained of intuition, perhaps, and that decision is not part of a sensual intuition nor of language. Sartre demands from the writer that he have something to say, which can only be measured in terms of a system of transcendent values. The writer, he says, must write as a man, responsible for what he writes and aiming at certain targets, not as a child, firing his weapon "at random, by shutting his eyes, and merely for the pleasure of hearing the shot go off" (15). Writing is an appeal to the liberty of another and cannot attempt to overwhelm the reader or to arouse in him fear, desire, or any state of passion. Literature cannot proceed by constraint or fascination, and consequently the only ultimately admissible style and technique in prose is directness. Writing must be divided into form and matter; for "good authors" form never precedes.

There remains unresolved in this discussion the question of a literary value of a text, which Sartre has not rejected. In the "Présentation des Temps modernes," his 1945 preface to the journal with which he has been associated for so many years, he proposes to publish texts on a basis that still considers their literary value, and that value is something extrinsic to their social intention. An "engaged" writer can yet be a mediocre one, he admits in *Qu'est-ce que la littérature?* "One is not a writer for having chosen to say certain things, but for having chosen to say them in a certain way. And, to be sure, the style makes the value of the prose. *But it should pass unnoticed.* . . . Beauty is in this case only a gentle and imperceptible force . . . in a book it hides itself, it acts by persuasion like the charm of a voice or a face. . . . In prose the aesthetic pleasure is pure only if it is thrown into the bargain" (16, my italics). To us, these ambiguous considerations are very little satisfactory. Making style subsidiary to content hardly demystifies literature, since it remains a form of illusion and persuasion. "In committed literature, *commitment* should at no time make us forget *literature*" (*Situations 2,* p. 30). This is Sartre's answer: the real value of a book lies in its total impact, not just in its political meaning. But still, what is the exact role of style within that impact? How can unnoticed style and beauty be allowed to persuade when literature must eschew fascination?

Sartre reproaches "pure" literature with its overemphasis on style, its predilection for words instead of thoughts, and its insistence on the merely personal. At base, he considers it a perversion of literature. "This is 'true,' 'pure' literature, a subjectivity which yields itself under the aspect of the objective, a discourse so curiously contrived that it is equivalent to silence, a thought which debates with itself, a reason which is only the mask of madness" (21). "Pure" literature expresses the cult of subjectivity; it transforms literature into a marketplace for "little straying souls" and the literary art into "the ensemble of treatments which render them inoffensive" (22). Tanned, refined, chemically treated, the souls of authors are made into objects that are to be contemplated from a respectful distance and whose use is guaranteed without risk.

This terrorist, antirhetorical attack on "pure" literature takes its place in *Qu'est-ce que la littérature?* within a more general attack on the tradition of French literature and on the bourgeois writer. Although the writer in France has been a perpetual antagonist of conservative forces, he has nonetheless, according to Sartre, always been a "parasite" of the ruling elite in society. He is an unproductive and dangerous luxury that the ruling classes have permitted themselves. As such, his work has been totally useless; he consumes and does not produce. Although the position of the writer is essentially a critical one, historically he has allowed his destructive power to be controlled by the elite, and he has written only for an elite public. Since the rise of bourgeois power, the writer—too "timid" to oppose his financial masters, who had closed around him like a prison—has allowed himself to be put into a position of particular inauthenticity:

> Idealism, psychologism, determinism, utilitarianism, the spirit of seriousness, that is what the bourgeois writer has to reflect to his public first of all. He is no longer asked to restore the strangeness and opacity of the world, but to dissolve it into elementary subjective impressions which make it easier to digest. . . . All his works are at once inventories of bourgeois appurtenances, psychological reports of an expert which invariably tend to ground the rights of the elite and to show the wisdom of institutions, and handbooks of civility. The conclusions are decided in advance; the psychological motives are selected, the very style is regulated. The public fears no surprise; it can buy with its eyes closed. But literature has been assassinated. [77]

Once prophet, pariah, *maudit,* the writer now grotesquely ranks among the specialists, with the stamp collectors and the weight lifters.

Sartre equates the parasitism of the bourgeois writer with cowardice and passivity. The subjectivism of contemporary literature means for Sartre a fear of the real world outside the writer and a passive turning in to the self. For the most, it reflects only self-pity and an insistence on the writer's vices, weaknesses, and unhappiness. There have been those, Sartre admits, who have refused this role and this conception of literature and who have courageously insisted on literature as negation. They have created the best in modern literature, but they, too, have slipped into error; in the end, the literature of destruction seems to Sartre a literature of adolescence. "Literature as absolute Negation becomes Anti-literature: the circle is completed" (89).

But there have been great writers. For Sartre they are the ones who wanted to destroy and to demonstrate, to contest and to construct, all at once. Sartre leaves aside the question of literary value to judge works great in terms of their efficacy and their ability to create change within their own societies; he measures the force of a writer by the direct action of his work on the public. Does a novel produce outrage, enthusiasm, or meditation in its readers? These are for Sartre the criteria of judgment. The correct function of the writer is not to let himself flow onto the page in "abject passivity," but to attack the world around him, to seize upon writing as an act. In an ideal classless society, the "concrete public would be an immense feminine questioning, the waiting of a whole society which the writer would have to seduce and satisfy" (105). In this active, masculine stance, writing becomes an act of sexual generosity, and the writer redeems himself by giving of himself.

For Sartre, the force of a work of art is measured first of all in terms of its social impact, the degree to which it creates a collective bad conscience; and it should not, therefore, be judged outside its concrete situation. No work of art can be reduced to bare ideas, since each creation is "totally penetrated by an existence," that is to say, characterized by freedom. The artist works on an unassimilable and irreducible material—language—that he can never completely ingest or integrate into a system, to create a work that reproduces both being and existence.

Style, then, becomes sensitivity to the material aspects

of language, directed with the intention of forcefully, gracefully, and efficiently producing a certain social result. Language is allusion and ellipsis within a given framework, and its use as style only has meaning within that framework. The work of art, which lifts society out of the "bog" of the immediate, reflects the material aspect of its medium; it includes elements of hardness, resistance, and moral austerity: "The bad novel aims to please by flattering, whereas the good one is an exigence and an act of faith" (40). Literature should be more than seduction; it should go beyond any appeal to the emotions (since the emotions are "degraded" forms of consciousness for Sartre) to argue and demonstrate, as an objective appeal to the "free" generosity of the reader. The goal of art is to "communicate with other men by modestly utilizing the available means" (*Situations 2,* p. 34); in contemporary society, however, that modest communication seems strangely enough to function almost as a rape of the consciousness, as it is necessarily marked by suddenness and violence. It is "no longer time to *describe* or to *narrate*": "When each word might cost a life, you ought not to take time off to play the cello. You go as fast as possible. You make it snappy" (162). In these terms, style can no longer be understood as a problematic tinkering with nuance and resonance; it can only imply a direct technique centered on praxis and on the object. "After Hemingway, how could we dream of describing? We must plunge things into action. Their density of being will be measured for the reader by the multiplicity of practical relations which they maintain with the characters. Have the mountain climbed by the smuggler, the customs officer, and the guerilla, have it flown over by the aviator, and the mountain will suddenly surge from these connected actions and jump out of your book like a jack-in-the-box. Thus, the world and man reveal themselves by undertakings. And all the undertakings we might speak of reduce themselves to a single one, that of *making history*" (165).

Sartre completes his attack on "pure" literature and the bourgeois writer with an attack on the cowardice of the contemporary critic. Critics, he says, were once people who liked to read; in the twentieth century, they have become merely the professional "chroniqueurs" of literature. In 1947, they have no humanistic interest in following the general line of an author's evolution; instead, they cut the work off from the author and busy themselves with classifications, labels, and predictions in their haste to make each author a recognized national resource. "Through fear and a taste for social consecration, critics read today the way one re-reads" (*Situations 2*, p. 44).

Sartre's point is that, as writing is an uncertain enterprise, so reading, for an author's contemporary, should share the risks of that enterprise; it should require the minimal naiveté that allows the reader to react honestly and immediately, to risk making his own evaluation of a book. But contemporary critics, he feels, are unsettled by new thoughts and new forms of expression, and they hasten to neutralize their effect on a passive public. With ill-concealed impatience they await the writer's death:

> It must be borne in mind that most critics are people who have not had much luck and who, just about the time they were growing desperate, found a quiet little job as cemetery watchmen. God knows that cemeteries are peaceful; none of them are more cheerful than a library. . . . The book, in effect, is by no means an object; neither is it an act, nor even a thought: written by a dead man about dead things, it no longer has any place on this earth; it speaks of

nothing which interests us directly. . . . It is a holi-
day for [the critic] when contemporary authors do him
the favor of dying: their books, too raw, too living, too
urgent, pass on to the other shore; they become less
and less affecting and more and more beautiful. . . .
Our critics are Cathars: they don't want to have anything to do with the real world except eat and drink in
it, and since it is absolutely necessary to have relations
with our fellow creatures, they have chosen to have
them with the defunct. They get excited only about
classified matters, closed quarrels, stories whose ends
are known. [17–19]

From *Situations 1* to *Situations 2,* through the creation
of *Les Temps modernes,* the urge towards schematic formulation and decree grows much stronger in Sartre. In the
articles on Parain and Renard he seemed to be testing and
clarifying his intuitions and preoccupations; by *Qu'est-ce
que la littérature?* he has integrated them into a fully developed approach. Along the way, he does much violence
to detail: from his arbitrary distinction between poetry
and prose and his circular argument that there is no good
anti-Semitic novel (based on his definition of "good" as an
appeal to freedom), to his roughshod trampling of a thousand years of French literature (from the medieval clerks
to his eighteenth-century heroes to 1947), Sartre keeps his
train of thought fluid by repeated, obsessive jumps in the
argument. The key to the development of *Qu'est-ce que la
littérature?* is a series of unproven assumptions, built on
attitudes we first met in the essay on Husserl. Here the
sensitivity to sexual dichotomies is expressed through the
dialectics of form and matter, life and death, the active
and the passive.

Sartre's position in *Situations 2,* where he argues for the

living and the active and against the feminine and the
passive in literature, can be understood, of course, in terms
of the general climate of opinion of the twentieth-century
French bourgeoisie. His feelings about femininity are
similar to the general attitude Beauvoir described in *Le
Deuxième Sexe* (though she has spoken elsewhere of Sartre's attitude towards women as "exemplary"); his political
approach is entirely reasonable for an ex-Resistance writer
of the left. But the weak points of his argument, and the
associated forcefulness of his style, bear very clearly
Sartre's personal mark. Throughout his career he will continue to rely on unprovable assumptions—they become too
numerous to list—and by *L'Idiot de la famille* he is forced
to protect himself by admitting the fabulous nature of
some of his reconstructions. What may be considered here
to directly reflect a climate of opinion eventually becomes
less and less recognizable: the political motivations of
Situations 2 develop into a negation of "normal" values in
Saint Genet; over the years, the theoretically derivative
sexual metaphor becomes increasingly similar to a metaphysical given. In dealing with Baudelaire, with the black
poets, and with Genet, Sartre's work grows more and more
personalized.

2

Baudelaire and *Black Orpheus*

Baudelaire

Quelques états d'âme truqués, quelques opérations sur le langage, ce n'est pas cela qui changera le cours du monde.

Saint Genet

At about the same time that he was working on *Qu'est-ce que la littérature?*, in his early forties, Sartre undertook an introduction to Baudelaire's *Ecrits Intimes*, in which he attempted to show that Baudelaire had chosen to live as he did and had had exactly the life he deserved. The result, *Baudelaire* (1947), was the first working, concrete example of Sartre's "existential psychoanalysis," which he had previously defined in theoretical terms in *L'Etre et le Néant*. The German phenomenologists are generally considered to be the sources of inspiration for *L'Etre et le Néant*, but in large measure the work is also a response to Freud, or to the Freudisms current in France at the time of its composition. In it Sartre claimed kinship with Freudian methodology. He, too, sought to analyze the profound intentional structures of every act, no matter how small (since each act has meaning and must be placed within the total context of the way I live in the world, each act is an expression of freedom, a rupture with the past), and he accepted the centrality of childhood, early trauma, neurosis, and the repetition of the original traumatic scene. But in 1943 Sartre could not accept Freud's theory of the unconscious (though he does today),[1] and he attacked Freud's

1. In 1975, he now appears to accept some form of the unconscious.

53

division of the subject's psychic unity into segments that are mutually ignorant and Freud's explanatory reduction of the mind into mechanisms. For Sartre, Freud's theories constituted a determinism, expressible in biological and physiological metalanguages. Sartre's opposition to all forms of determinism is a moral one, and it lies at the heart of his philosophy of freedom. The division of the mind into conscious will and unconscious passion allows me to deny responsibility for my acts, but for Sartre, man must feel the responsibility for each of his acts at every moment. He therefore replaced the hypothesis of the unconscious with that of *mauvaise foi*. By this Sartre means a lie I tell myself, of which I am conscious, and which rests on the denial that a human being is a free self-making process. Mauvaise foi is an effort to disguise my own freedom and to make myself into an object. Secondly, Sartre began to work toward an existential psychoanalysis that would correct Freud by viewing acts as symbolizing and reaffirming a free original choice, a "choice of being" synonymous with freedom and consciousness; that is, a choice of values and perspectives, a way of "living my body" and "facticity" (my relation to my world and my past), and a projection of the self into the future. My project is the outline of a solution to the problem of being.

According to Beauvoir, Gide, the surrealists, even Freud, have taught Sartre and her that in each person there exists what Breton called "an unbreakable kernel of night." Sartre himself now admits the unconscious as a "total absence of knowledge but real comprehension," that is, a nonobjective, immediate intuition. On this basis he admits Freudian disguise and repression through the trick of forgetfulness and he acknowledges that he cannot account rationally for those processes that are "below" consciousness and that are also rational, but lived as irrational. While Sartre still sees psychoanalytic theory as syncretic, not based on dialectical rigor, and therefore "molle" (soft), he remains nonetheless a fellow-traveler, as he once described himself. See "Sartre par Sartre," in *Situations 9,* and Arnold and Piriou, *Les Mots de Sartre,* pp. 20–23.

In this light each act must be understood in view of original ends, defined by a possibility; and the analysis of acts must be oriented towards the future as well as the past.

To Sartre, then, Baudelaire lived exactly as he wanted, or, rather, he chose to experience the limits of his situation in a certain way, and he is to be held responsible for the meaning of his life. His "destiny," his premature death, his syphilis, his dependent financial status, his avaricious mistress, his relations with his mother—there is not one circumstance of his life of which he is not the author, for which he is not "fully and lucidly responsible." He maps out the geography and weaves the text of his miserable life, according to the fashion in which he chooses to view his world.

In some ways, *Baudelaire* ought not to be such a bitter pill to swallow. Its message is humanistic, if vindictive. It is less rigid, less elaborate and repetitive, more human in its jealous spitefulness than the awesomely brilliant but abstract, graceless comprehension and arid self-indictment of *Saint Genet*. Yet, for many, if not most, critics *Baudelaire* remains an unmitigated disaster, and the critical attack on this essay over the last twenty-five years has been unending.

What the critics first hold against Sartre is that he seems out to "get" Baudelaire. Georges Blin has spoken of *Baudelaire* as an abusive indictment; for Philip Thody it is a "moral cautionary tale," full of "implicit self-satisfaction"; for Georges Bataille, an "act of moral aggression directed against poetry in general . . . he speaks to us of the poet with the intention of doing away with him." [2] More than

2. Georges Blin, "Jean-Paul Sartre et Baudelaire," *Fontaine* 11, no. 59 (April, 1947): 200-216; Philip Thody, *Jean-Paul Sartre: A Literary and Political Study* (New York: Macmillan, 1960), p. 140; Georges Bataille, "Baudelaire 'mis à nu,'" *Critique* 8-9 (January, 1947): 3-27.

one critic has listed the consistently denigrating terms
Sartre applies to Baudelaire:

> . . . pervers, obsédé, morne indifférent, indélicat fri-
> sant parfois l'escroquerie, masochiste, antisémite,
> voyeur, dédaigneux, artificiel, frisant le ridicule, tru-
> queux, fétichiste, vicieux, monstrueux, menteur, mani-
> aque, onanistement avare, falsificateur subtil, prostitué,
> exhibitionniste, hystérique, il annonce Barrès, on l'a
> dit impuissant . . .[3]

There are, too, stylistic affectations that mock Baudelaire's
effeminateness, negative comparisons with Sartrian heroes
(Gide, Nietzsche, Rimbaud), simplistic approximations,
laughable "pearls" of philosophy, and bad scholarship.
Sartre contextually distorts citations; he concentrates on
casual remarks while ignoring whole elaborated texts on
the same subjects; he takes at face value the deliberate
mystifications and jokes of the journals, and uses the cor-
respondence as irrefutable evidence, apparently never
questioning the sincerity of the letters or the literary pose
implicit in them. In sum, for many the work is a "vie
romancée," a popular, fictionalized biography. Sartre
himself has referred to his study of Baudelaire as "very in-
sufficient, very bad, even,"[4] but for evidently different
reasons; for Sartre today, the main fault of *Baudelaire*
would be its failure to situate its subject within a social
and historical context.

The principal arguments of Sartre's critics, aside from
those who argue with his definition of liberty or his
ambiguous use of the concept, are that his critique is
anachronistic and "imperialistic," that Baudelaire is con-

---

3. See Louis Jourdain, "Sartre devant Baudelaire," *Tel Quel* 19 (Autumn,
1964): 70-85; 21 (Spring, 1965): 79-95.
4. *Situations 9*, p. 113.

demned for actions for which Genet is praised, and that
Baudelaire's "failure" is the source of a creative liberation,
of which Sartre offers no account. By "imperialistic" criticism the critics have meant that Sartre neglects Baudelaire's
Catholicism and forces his own system of metaphysics, his
own obsessions and perceptions of life, onto Baudelaire's
ethics. Beyond that, his language, through the automatic
association of certain images with certain themes, distorts
his argument and his portrait of Baudelaire: he reduces
Baudelaire to an abstraction. Sartre seems to show no
understanding of the beauty, creative significance, truth,
and authenticity of Baudelaire's poetry. In Thody's words,
rather than the creative artist that Baudelaire was, Sartre
would have preferred him to be a "third-rate socialist pam-
phleteer": Sartre attacks Baudelaire for being Baudelaire.
   Michel Leiris, Sartre's prefacer (who has been spoken of
as Sartre's dupe), has defended *Baudelaire* on the grounds
that it is not literary criticism but an exercise in existential
psychoanalysis, with the limited literary intention of offer-
ing a key to the "fait poétique" of Baudelaire. He is, of
course, quite correct. More recently, Benjamin Suhl has
somewhat astonishingly seen Sartre's essay as "the only
monument possible" to Baudelaire and claims that Sartre
has discovered the "secret" of Baudelaire's poetry.[5] Actually, there is very little in *Baudelaire* in the way of
concrete analysis of the poetry (since, for the most, the
poems are used, deliberately, as biographical documents).
Sartre makes a few remarks about the "ineffable grace" of
the poetry, develops briefly the problematic relationship
of subjectivity and objectivity for the poet, and, in his
most important and incisive contribution, explains Baudelaire's "fait poétique" (poetic reality) by the "spirituality"
of the poems, brilliantly commenting at the same time on

5. *Jean-Paul Sartre*, p. 149.

the importance of perfumes and of the past in *Les Fleurs du Mal.* One must admit that the book is not literary criticism, in any standard sense (though the best of it is, as the best of *L'Idiot de la famille* to date consists of fitfully brilliant analyses of Flaubert's juvenilia and of scenes from *Madame Bovary*).

Nevertheless, the thrust of the attack on *Baudelaire* remains valid. To more than one critical generation, to more than a few careful readers, Baudelaire's poetry has appeared at least as total and authentic as would that of the Antillean poet Aimé Césaire, for example; yet Sartre refuses to consider it, as he does consider Césaire's poetry, in the light of a creative liberation or totalization. In *Saint Genet* genius is explained as "the way out one invents in desperate cases"; in *Baudelaire* Sartre ignores the problem of the liberating *issue* of the poet by refusing to admit or consider his genius. Both Genet and Baudelaire take up the attitudes of sulky children. Neither one rejects the moral code of the people who raised them, but Genet's *bouderie* becomes the expression of a man's liberty because it is at the origin of "the most singular, the most beautiful of poetic achievements"; since Baudelaire is apparently only the author of a few charming poems, his equivalent defense has only the dignity of a simple infantile reaction. Somehow, Baudelaire is guilty of a choice of which Sartre does not approve, while Genet is to be pitied as a victim of society. Baudelaire, who received the affective shock of rejection that led to his original choice at the age of seven-and-a-half, deserves no sympathy; Genet, who discovers his "eternal essence" when found stealing at age ten, should touch our hearts as "a child who has been caught, a very young child" (31), who has been trapped like a rat by society and turned into a "monster."

What are the sources of Sartre's irritation with Baudelaire?

As made clear above, Sartre presents as his goal in *Baude-laire* an application of existential psychoanalysis: he will prove through Baudelaire that what one calls "destiny" identifies absolutely with the free choice a man makes of himself; through Baudelaire he will pinpoint mauvaise foi and the reality of man's impossible desire to be an object for his own eyes. These aims are consistently apparent in *Baudelaire,* it is true, but their demonstration need not have implied any rejection of Baudelaire himself, who is really only an example of the impossible condition of all men, and of the fact stated in *L'Etre et le Néant* that all lives are failures. There is an obvious political motivation in attacking Baudelaire as a parasite of bourgeois society, but Sartre's antipathy seems rooted in something prior even to this polemic approach. Even Baudelaire's mauvaise foi could be treated without the particularly peevish tone that Sartre adopts; the implicit resentment is external to Sartre's argument, it is personal. The emotional function of Sartre's language, the jagged strain of impatience with Baudelaire, the annoyance that this man should receive such undeserved pity and sympathy, are directed at, or stem from, not only Baudelaire's social position, but also the specific content of Baudelaire's choice and behavior: the argument based on Baudelaire's dissimulation of his own freedom reduces to an attack on his refusal to become a man.[6]

What Sartre has against Baudelaire is that, in Sartre's eyes, he never grows up. He never rejects his mother or any

6. As we shall see, Flaubert, too, never grows up, according to Sartre. The same problem confronts Mathieu in *L'Age de raison* and Hugo in *Les Mains sales.* The decision to choose a path for the future takes one out of the natural "sweet confusion" of childhood and forces one into an adult world of responsi-bility. That world is problematic: all of *L'Age de raison* seems to revolve around a group of individuals in their thirties (Mathieu, Marcelle, Lola, Daniel), who are trying for a "last chance" to keep their youth and "freedom," and their relations with others who are still young and unattached (Boris, Ivich).

form of parental authority, never gives his brilliance a masculine thrust that would liberate him; he refuses the evident conclusions of his lucidity so as to deny his future and his liberty. His life is an act of inauthenticity, a defense against his own freedom and responsibility. In sum, he is an unmanly coward. "Baudelaire is no more than a marionette whose strings are being manipulated."[7]

As a child, according to Sartre's hypothesis, Baudelaire experiences the world as an extension of the moist intimacy of the self, which is supported by the gentle warmth of maternal love and justification. He lives in sacred union with his widowed mother; she is his idol, and he is "son by divine right," consecrated and justified by their union, totally absorbed in her necessary existence, totally penetrated by the religion of their unanimity, protected and sheltered in her embrace. When his mother remarries, he experiences the remarriage as a rejection, and the damp closeness of their life "had gone out like a tide, leaving him alone, high and dry" (17). The brusque rupture of their life throws him into the discovery of a personal existence: he finds himself alone, separate and singular, exposed to the eyes of others, and condemned to solitude. In discovering his singularity, he discovers that he is *un autre;* he feels himself as set apart and senses that others see him as different, but he cannot himself seize or see this difference. To see himself as others see him, to protect himself from their eyes, he defiantly exaggerates the rejection, the separation, imposed upon him; he refuses to accept it passively, but instead affirms it as a choice. He pursues his otherness; he demands to be noticed as different, as other, he demands to be judged.

Later in his life, after his stepfather's death, he makes of

7. *Baudelaire,* trans. Martin Turnell (Norfolk, Conn.: James Laughlin, 1950), p. 161. References in the text are to this translation.

his mother—the only person for whom he ever felt tenderness, whom he loves more as a woman than as a mother,
who remains associated for him with a sweet and free
childhood—a severe and unchallengeable judge. "She
possessed neither the strength nor the inclination to
punish him, yet he trembled in front of this insignificant
little woman whom he knew through and through" (62).
He invests her with the supreme power to judge him; he
hopes to find in her final judgment his salvation, the consecration of his life. He transfers to her the role and authority
of the father, partly because of his incestuous love for her,
more because of his need for authority.

At a certain point, Sartre says, every child grows old
enough to look over his parents' shoulders and to discover
that behind their authority there is nothing. He discovers
then his own transcendence, freedom, and responsibility;
his parents shrink, they appear "thin and mediocre, unjus-
tifiable, unjustified" (53), and all the certainties of his life
disappear. "He suddenly finds that the world has to be
remade. All the places and even the order of things are dis-
puted; and since he is no longer a thought in a divine
Reason, since the look which fixed him is no more than a
tiny light among other tiny lights, the child loses his essence
and his truth. . . . Everything still has to begin. He suddenly emerges in solitude and the void" (53–54).

It is precisely this experience, the discovery and recognition of solitude and responsibility, that Baudelaire refuses
to accept: "It could be argued that he never progressed
beyond the stage of childhood" (52). As Sartre understands
it, Baudelaire has looked over his parents' shoulders, seen
emptiness, and refused it. He hides his liberty from himself
because it frightens him. "The law of solitude might, indeed, be expressed in these terms: No man can place on
others the burden of justifying his existence. It was precisely

this that terrified Baudelaire. Solitude filled him with horror. . . . And it will be realized that it was not a question of physical isolation, but of the 'emergence in the void' which was the price of uniqueness" (61-62).

Baudelaire is therefore to be branded a coward. Afraid of solitude, afraid of autonomy, he retreats from his lucidity into a world of mauvaise foi. In search of his own otherness, frightened by his own liberty, he seeks on the one hand a solitude that terrifies him on the other. He defends himself from the condemning gaze of the Other by seeking to inspire horror in the Other. It is especially his parents who must judge and condemn him, it is his parents he must horrify, and through them he has no need to create his own meaning and order in emptiness. His parents remain for him "hateful idols," but still idols. He resents them, he knows well the catalogue of their faults, the absurdity of their power and morality, but he never challenges their authority, nor the principles by which they judge him. Had he done so, he would have been freed, "but he took good care not to: he adopted the moral code of his stepfather without questioning it" (46).

He takes up the defiant attitude of a sulky child "who stamps his feet and exaggerates his faults" (47). His attitude is not that of revolution but of rebellion: "The rebel is careful to preserve the abuses from which he suffers so he can go on rebelling against them" (51-52). He tries not to destroy established moral norms nor to create boldly his own system of values, but seeks instead to be punished and judged within the given system. He does this in perfect mauvaise foi; knowing exactly the arbitrariness of the system imposed upon him and the extent of his own freedom, he hides that freedom from his own view and accepts the judgment of a bourgeois world. He presents himself as in revolt against the moral system that he refuses to destroy.

He never ceases to look for judges. In his parents, in the substitutes offered as parental authorities, Baudelaire continues to find absolute authority and absolute justification. As long as there is an authority to judge him, an eye to watch him, he has his place and his meaning. "The pariah was banned by society, but precisely because in this way he became the object of a social act his solitude was consecrated and even necessary to the proper functioning of institutions" (55). In a world of "those who whip" and "those who are whipped," he chooses to be the latter, because beyond the "whipper" there is only emptiness.

In a sense, I understand this essay to say that Baudelaire chooses to desiccate himself. The moist intimacy of his early life is torn apart by his mother's remarriage, and he is left "seul et sec." He chooses to affirm both his imposed solitude and his imposed dryness by making of himself an arid, sterile, metallic, solid object, by destroying whatever is natural in himself. But despite all his self-manipulation in the direction of stiffness and density, pattern and order, Baudelaire stands condemned, Sartre maintains, because, unlike Genet, but like Flaubert, he cannot go "all the way," and he never succeeds in eradicating within himself a secret remnant of his original, shapeless fluidity. "The basic distance between Baudelaire and the world was not the same as ours. In his case we are aware of something translucent, slightly damp and rather too highly perfumed, which insinuated itself between the man and his object like the vibration of the warm air in summer" (23).[8] What this means is that Sartre sees Baudelaire as bent over his own

8. What is "our" distance from the world? The use of the first person plural is fascinating here, because with it Sartre seems to set up a standard of conformity with which to condemn Baudelaire. In his other prefaces and in *Saint Genet* the "we" is self-accusatory: we are the bourgeois who abuse Genet. See Jacques Ehrmann, "Of Rats and Men: Notes on the Prefaces," *Yale French Studies*, no. 30 (1964): 78–85.

reflection, like Narcissus, working on his own image, con-
tracting himself, bridling himself, hardening himself into
an object, in a defensive movement toward masculinity,
toward the rigid concentration of the dandy, but never
succeeding in purifying himself of the feminine element
within him, symbolized by an oozing, formless wetness.
His well-known characteristics—dandyism, frigidity, antinaturalism—are all defenses against the threatening flow of
femininity within him, but insofar as they fall short of
revolution they are equally defenses against his own liberty
and against the Other, mere pretenses of revolt. So, Baudelaire's cult of the frigid, his image of himself as sterile,
gratuitous, and pure, protects him, in Sartre's view, against
both an amorphous, overly abundant, vegetable world, and
a "warm, soft, mucous life" (117). (The relation between
this and Roquentin's view of the world has been pointed
out frequently.) His artificialism, his hatred of the common, the spontaneous, the immediate, the natural, his
attraction to metal, light, and transparence, at once aim to
preserve his singularity against biological determinism and
to defend him against an internal feminine fertility that
disgusts him:

> Above everything else, he had a horror of feeling this
> vast, soft fecundity in himself. . . . When he felt na-
> ture—the nature which belonged to everybody—rising
> and taking possession of him like a flood, he went rigid
> and taut holding his head above the water. The great
> muddy wave was vulgarity itself. Baudelaire was irri-
> tated when he felt inside him the clammy waves which
> were so unlike the subtle combinations of which he
> had dreamed; he was irritated above all by the feeling
> that this soft, irresistible power wanted to make him
> compliant, make him "do the same as everybody else."

. . . Baudelaire chose not to be nature, to be the perpetual jarring refusal of his "natural self," the head that
stuck out of the water, watching it rise with a mixture
of terror and disdain. [109-10]

As Baudelaire's artificialism serves to purify himself of
the natural and the fertile within him, so his dandyism intends to cleanse him of femininity. The search for hardness
that Sartre focuses on in Baudelaire could represent only a
symbolization of man's quest for essential being (and this
is how most critics understand it) except that in this case
Sartre gives it more specific reference. Baudelaire stiffens
himself into dandyism because dandyism for him constitutes the ceremonial, concentrated essence of virility,
because it opposes itself directly to *veulerie, abandon,
détente,* because the dandy negates the woman. "Woman
is an inferior animal, a 'latrine,' she 'is in heat and wants to
be poked'; she is the opposite of the dandy" (119).

All of these defenses are failures, as Baudelaire's life is a
failure, because, Sartre believes, it is not possible for
Baudelaire to rid himself of his femininity through dandyism or antinaturalism. He cannot choose to be entirely
masculine in any one form of specific action because his
original choice is of femininity: he does not succeed because he never rejects his mother. Baudelaire "will be fixed
all his life on his mother."[9] Where the proper Sartrian hero
would break forth from maternal constraint and stride
boldly forth into the world to reconquer his name and his
heritage, Baudelaire remains tamely and securely at home,
tied to his mother in every way, refusing to grow up. He
may change her image to masculinize her, to make her into
a judge, but Sartre claims that he has internalized her

9. *Search for a Method,* trans. Hazel E. Barnes (New York: Knopf, 1963),
p. 63.

earlier meaning. He has incorporated within himself the familiar dampness of their early union and remains always marked by the maternal influence, undeveloped in relation to reality, arrested in the process of becoming a man. He remains fixed upon his past self and he looks only for traces of his own intimate self in reality; his life, a vain attempt at self-recuperation and self-clarification, is stagnant and unchanging, passive and feminine. His dandyism, ostensible virility, is a product of guilt and timidity; a complication of his original choice that expresses the contradictions of his original choice, it is a denial of femininity that expresses femininity:

> There was in Baudelaire a scarcely perceptible passage from the virility of dandyism to a sort of feminine coquettishness, to a feminine taste for clothes. . . . We can see that it suggests the pederast rather than the dandy. [147–48]

> It has seemed a matter of surprise that he sometimes looked like a woman and certain writers have tried to discover in him signs of a homosexuality of which he never showed any trace. But we must remember that "femineity" comes from a person's condition, not from his sex. The essential characteristic of woman—of the bourgeois woman—is that she depends very largely on *opinion*. She is idle and kept. She asserts herself by pleasing; she dresses in order to please; clothes and makeup serve partly to reveal and partly to conceal her. Any man who happened to find himself in a similar condition would probably assume an appearance of "femineity." This was Baudelaire's position. He did not earn his living by working which meant that the money on which he lived was not remuneration for some social service which could be appreciated objectively,

> but depended essentially on people's judgments of
> him. Yet his initial choice of himself implied an extra-
> ordinary, a constant concern for opinion. He knew
> that he was seen; he knew that people's eyes were con-
> tinually on him; he wanted to please and displease at
> the same time. His least gesture was "for the public."
> His pride was hurt by it, but his masochism rejoiced in
> it. When he went out dressed up to the eyes, it was a
> regular ceremony. He had to look after his clothes, hop
> over puddles, preserve all those defensive gestures,
> which were a little ridiculous, by investing them with a
> certain grace. And the gaze which enveloped him was
> there. While he was going gravely through the thousand
> impotent little gestures which belonged to his priestly
> office, he felt that he was penetrated, *possessed* by
> other people. It was not by his bearing and his strength,
> not by the external signs of a social function that he
> tried to defend himself, to assert himself; it was by his
> dress and by the grace of his movements. [152-53]

Baudelaire's dandyism as self-sufficiency is a myth, it is a
daily renewed compensation for his thinglike passivity, for
his exhibitionist's prostitution before the crowd.

Baudelaire's most important defense, whose putative
failure makes his life a "failure," an experience within
closed walls, is the mask he places over his own freedom,
his refusal of the future. In one sense, even this mechanism
is considered by Sartre in the light of Baudelaire's femininity. Sartre accuses Baudelaire of retreating into the past,
disguising immediate reality, and making his life gratuitous
and without real effect. Baudelaire refuses to challenge the
world around him. Baudelairian dissatisfaction (nonsatis-
faction) is too vague for Sartre, too concretely accepting,
too little aggressive. But in the abdication of responsibility,

the cowardice, that Sartre decries in Baudelaire, Baudelaire himself, and many others, saw a positive affirmation, an "obedience to that which is," which he experienced to the fullest as necessary for the creation of the greatest art. *Perinde ac cadaver:* only thus are cathedrals built. Sartre contemptuously rejects this credo; he refuses to see in it an act of Nietzschean affirmation, but reduces it instead to timorous passivity, to femininity. In *L'Idiot de la famille* Sartre denies the possibility of obedience as a choice of authentic action: "The act—even as the result of an order— is a form of sovereignty: this means that it comprises an inexplicit negation of obedience."[10] Baudelaire's creative act, then, can only be understood by Sartre as a product of cowardice and inauthenticity. Wanting, like Rimbaud, to be a "radical creator" (182), to create himself, he becomes frightened by total responsibility and solitude, he does not have the courage to continue, and his art becomes per- fumed theatrics:

> Rimbaud didn't waste his time working up a horror of nature; he simply smashed it like a money-box. Baude- laire smashed nothing at all. His work as a creator merely consisted in the travestying and the ordering of things. He accepted all the suggestions which came from his spontaneous consciousness. He simply wanted to touch them up a little, forcing them here, toning them down there. He was not going to indulge in roars of laughter when he felt like crying. He would weep "more truly than nature." That was all. The conclusion of his act would be the poem which would offer him the image —rethought, recreated and objectified—of the emotion which he had half felt. Baudelaire was a pure creator of form; Rimbaud created form and matter. [158-59]

10. *L'Idiot de la famille* (Paris: Gallimard, 1971), vol. 1, p. 49.

This last sentence of this passage is almost indefensible; by this point in his argument Sartre has abandoned any real effort at objective confirmation of his viewpoint. Take it or leave it: in most readers of Baudelaire the response is immediate negation of Sartre's argument. The picture of Rimbaud, too, here and in *Saint Genet,* is simplistic and sensational. In the end, one has to admit that to accuse Baudelaire of inauthenticity, to define his life as a failure, is a dishonest procedure, conceived in mauvaise foi. Sartre must know this; he must be aware of what he is not saying in order to make a point: that Baudelaire's choice ultimately is as viable as Genet's, that, dialectically, obedience to the given becomes an act, that the refusal of authenticity in acts is somehow necessary to Baudelaire's full, *inner* development, and that this sorry, ordinary, human performance is merely the obverse of a creative genius.

Here Sartre will not admit these possibilities because he wants to forge an identifying link between feminine passivity, bavardage, homosexuality, and *form.* There is something too "perfumed," too "adoring," about Baudelaire for Sartre; he communicates nothing to Sartre, and Sartre has to prove that he has nothing to say to anyone. Baudelaire has no poetic genius for him; his poetic work is mere simpering reorganization of the given and insincerely personal, "the travestying and the ordering of things." In *Baudelaire* the bourgeois moralist in Sartre has to deal with a marginally homoerotic, or androgynous, poetry of tenderness and vulnerability, and he refuses it as he refuses his own childhood. In *Saint Genet* he will have to deal with homosexuality face to face.

Mallarmé and *Black Orpheus*

In the first part of his career, Sartre's criticism is marked by an aggressive rigidity of interpretation and taste that remains of doubtful value. It is usually clear in these early essays that Sartre's critical judgment stems not only from an intuitive reading of a text for itself or from a consistent logical basis, but also from a direct reaction to the man he thinks he perceives behind a text. Over the years those reactions have demonstrated remarkably little sympathy for writers different from Sartre. For Sartre, the issue has always been to use the text to understand the man; on that basis he has strewn throughout his work arbitrary and one-sided assertions, acts of accusation and assassination, which seem irritatingly inconsistent with his normal lucidity and with the depth of his resources.

At one time or another Sartre has rejected Baudelaire as a "pure creator of form," Flaubert as an irresponsible bourgeois, and Proust as a homosexual and a mechanistic psychologist, without recognizing that they are all much more than that. In *Qu'est-ce que la littérature?* he attacked, among others, realists and surrealists, medieval clerks and contemporary bourgeois littérateurs, all in one long breath. In contrast, he has provisionally embraced such authors as Dos Passos, Fanon, Merleau-Ponty, Ponge, and even Gide on occasion, in terms that have seemed even, consistent, and understanding of the texts he treats. But his unbending rejection of Baudelaire and Proust is completed by an equivalently inadequate characterization of Rimbaud, whom he admires. It is not true that Baudelaire created nothing but form; neither is it true that Rimbaud represents only the masculine aspects of creativity or that his poetic technique fundamentally negates analogy, as Sartre will claim in *Saint Genet.*[11]

11. I have summarized his arguments below, in the section on *Saint Genet.* Sartre can justify his view of Rimbaud only by ignoring a number of significant texts. In the "Bateau ivre," for example, Rimbaud compares himself to "Une femme à genoux"; in *Une Saison en enfer,* he says, "L'action n'est pas la

There are, however, two essays written toward the end of this period (1948-53) in which Sartre tentatively moves towards a more generous attitude: his essay on Mallarmé (reprinted as a preface to Mallarmé's collected poems) and his introduction to contemporary black poetry, entitled "Orphée noir." [12] The essay on Mallarmé, published in 1953, is of particular interest in that it is extremely condensed. According to Beauvoir, Sartre has written, and discarded, hundreds of pages on Mallarmé, but the preface to the *Poésies* comes to no more than a few short pages.

Sartre expresses more ambivalence about Mallarmé, on a more intense level, than about perhaps any other writer. He cannot immediately deal with Mallarmé in a simple way: "Hero, prophet, magus, and tragedian, this little feminine man, discreet, scarcely drawn to women, merits dying at the threshold of our century: he announces it" (200). For Sartre, Mallarmé is the greatest French poet, and he is, on one level, exactly what a writer should be; that is, passionate, violent, a consciously committed revolutionary hero who would contest the entire world through a polite terrorism. His commitment can be understood as social as well as poetic; his poems are exploding bombs; his violence is so complete and desperate that, on a metaphysical level, the truth of his poems becomes *le néant*.

---

vie, mais une façon de gâcher quelque force." He uses analogy constantly in his poetry; the precise image Sartre discusses in *Saint Genet* is written: "L'Aube exaltée ainsi qu'un peuple de colombes."

12. Reprinted as "Mallarmé" in *Situations 9,* pp. 191-202; "Orphée noir," reprinted in *Situations 3* (Paris: Gallimard, 1949), pp. 229-86. The Mallarmé article appeared a few months after *Saint Genet,* though it resulted from the research of 1948-49. "Orphée noir" has been translated by S. W. Allen as *Black Orpheus* (Présence Africaine, n.d.); page references will be to that translation, with some changes. For both essays, page references will follow in the text.

Sartre particularly appreciates in Mallarmé his metaphysical anguish and revolt. After the death of God, the poet wants to produce out of pure matter an order superior to matter, he wants to replace God, and, of course, he fails; Mallarmé realizes this failure as a total commitment. But here Sartre's admiration falters. The problem he sees with Mallarmé's revolt is that it becomes an "alibi" to separate him from reality. According to Sartre, Mallarmé wants to explode the world, but, unlike the heroes of a number of Sartre's plays, without "dirtying his hands."

In this remark lies the core of Sartre's ambivalence: for Sartre, Mallarmé is essentially a feminine being. At this point Sartre cannot easily reconcile his image of the committed writer with "this little feminine man," this "sad trickster" (199). Mallarmé is neither manly enough nor direct enough to please Sartre. Unfortunately, this view of Mallarmé, only hinted at in the article, is extensively elaborated in *Saint Genet,* where Mallarmé is seen as purely feminine, the exact opposite of Rimbaud, and in *L'Idiot de la famille,* where citations from Mallarmé are used crudely and negatively in an effort to cast him as the final result, almost the pathological limit, of an "erroneous" aesthetic theory that Sartre "denounces." According to Sartre in volume 3 of *L'Idiot,* Mallarmé does not have the boldness to attack reality directly. Instead he pretends to ignore it, and escapes into an inactive dream that hides his metaphysical despair; he shares a "black religion" with Flaubert; he perfects Flaubert's techniques of "derealization" so as to radicalize failure, pessimism, the impossibility and the feminization of literature; he sums up a generation of literary neurosis, and, as we shall see later, he is one of the last—as well as the hero and theoretician—of a group of "black" writers in the second half of the nineteenth century whom Sartre calls the "knights of

Nothingness." What this last means is that from Flaubert to Mallarmé, Sartre discerns the presence of an unhealthy and perverted conception of literature, based on the idea of an aristocracy of nothingness and on nervous illness. Sartre struggles at length in *L'Idiot* to establish the communion and solidarity of this group and to make clear how much he deplores their influence. Particularly interesting in this respect is the fact that, for Sartre, Mallarmé, with Flaubert, fathers modern literature: since Mallarmé and Flaubert, poetry and prose have become "critical," that is, self-reflective, expressive of their own creation. Modern literature, in Sartre's view, though apparently healthier than the works of Mallarmé, is still in need of curative treatment; post-romantic literature, he believes, is an aberration from the "glory" of Voltaire and Rousseau, whose writing was properly negative, concrete, practical, and a continual struggle for autonomy. In the nineteenth century, with the triumph of the bourgeoisie, the work of art becomes its own end, negativity is transformed into absolute negation, and the writer expresses only a perpetual (and Baudelairian) dissatisfaction, an arid rejection of everything for nothing.

This is of interest because with the advent of *la nouvelle critique* and *le nouveau roman* over the last two decades, Sartre has shown himself increasingly interested in writing as a reflexive, self-conscious act, the "invention" of the self. Without going as far forward as his most recent work (*Plaidoyer pour les intellectuels* or his preface to André Puig's "critical novel"), we may take as an example the 1958 article on André Gorz, where Sartre speaks of "a work in the process of creating its own author." After Mallarmé, Sartre says, after the death of God and the disintegration of bourgeois society and of the illusion of reality, art is *necessarily* critical. This development of

Sartre's thought makes his judgment of Proust, who can be approached precisely along these lines, seem even more hasty and inadequate. Again, it is in these terms that he praises Nathalie Sarraute (*Situations 4*, pp. 9-16)—the honesty of her work, its sudden, brusque authenticity, is born, he suggests, in a contestation of the novel that becomes a "dévoilement" of human reality—and Michel Butor (*Situations 9*, p. 17), both "new" novelists. This praise is voiced despite his earlier attack on the new novelists and his even earlier attack on Nabokov and others as too literary and self-conscious.

In the few years between *Baudelaire* and *Saint Genet*, Mallarmé's loss is Genet's gain. In the preface to Mallarmé's poetry and in "Orphée noir" Sartre begins to realize that there actually are a "thousand ways" of being creative, and that they are perhaps of comparable value. Even Gide, whose ideas Sartre considers dated, is of value to Sartre as a writer because he lived his ideas to the end. In *Saint Genet*, only Mallarmé suffers from Sartre's antipathy for the feminine, which leaves Genet entirely sympathetic.

The introduction Sartre wrote in 1948 to Leopold Sedar Senghor's *Anthologie de la nouvelle poésie nègre et malgache* demands consideration as an important piece of criticism and as an acknowledged step forward in the history of negritude. "Orphée noir," composed in a distinctly recognizable blend of humility and stinging polemic, guilt and accusation, represents a particular form of Sartrian criticism at its best. Sartre attains in "Orphée noir" the emotional and literary level of *Saint Genet* and succeeds where he failed in *Baudelaire*. The essay is an appeal and an accusation, a commitment and an imaginative liberation that in large measure fulfills Sartre's own ambitiously defined ideals for prose. While one may regret the warmer, gentler author of *Les Mots,* one cannot but admire here the searing intensity of the poetic Sartre, as he reaches towards Roquentin's ideal literature, whose knifestrokes were to make people ashamed of their existence.

Sartre's ideas seem more convincingly alive in "Orphée noir" than elsewhere, partly because lengthy repetitions are cut down, complex demonstrations are elided, and the language remains clear and direct, but mostly because Sartre the professional philosopher gives way to Sartre the artist. What he tried to do in the essay on Husserl—to give life to ideas through poetic perception and emotional shading—he accomplishes rather more fully here, because in this quickly assembled and somewhat inaccurate piece he succeeds in joining his own hazily disordered and half-rejected perceptions to the larger, more poetically basic, and undeniably immediate rhythms of black poetry. He manages at once to remain reasonably faithful to the poetry he is dealing with and to his own intuition and, at the same time, to go far beyond the scope of the individual poem and perception. He is in love with this poetry and with the opportunity it gives him to speak out for the oppressed; and the depth of his emotion and sensitivity smooths over the occasional rough edges of his arbitrariness to make "Orphée noir," like *Saint Genet,* almost as valuable a literary experience as the material it treats. And, like Genet's own writing, the fullness of its commitment demands an equal involvement on the part of the reader.

What the critics have considered important in "Orphée noir" are the changes in Sartre's theories of literature, notably changes concerning the theoretical irresponsibility of poetry and the surrealist approach to language.[13] We have seen that in earlier essays Sartre consistently attacked

13. See Michel Beaujour, "Sartre and Surrealism," in *Yale French Studies,* no. 30 (1964): 63–67.

surrealism and its attempt to destroy language. "The great
surrealist prattling, which consisted in large measure in
crashing words without objects one against the other"
(*Situations 1*, p. 233), led nowhere, Sartre argued, but to
useless, pointless failure. The self-destruction of language
cannot return man to any original infrasilence; once the
curtain of words is ripped down, we find nothing behind
it. In "Orphée noir" Sartre first continues this argument:
the imaginative attempt to eradicate language should have
no effect on the real world. Reality stubbornly resists the
inroads of imagination, and thus European surrealism of
the twentieth century, falsely impersonal and objective,
remained only symbolic destruction and led only to
quietism.

But at this point in his argument Sartre makes a fascinating reversal. Senghor's anthology shows him new possibilities for surrealism, new relations between poetry and
reality. The black poets, using the surrealist method, have
recuperated the meaning and function of surrealism; they
have completed it and made it work. Aimé Césaire, for
example, has given surrealism its definitive sense and
turned it against the whites as a "rigorously prescribed
function" (39). The difference between European surrealism and black surrealism is that for the black poet "it is
not a question of a gratuitous game" (30). The situation
of the black poet reshapes surrealism. The European
surrealist's destruction remained only symbolic because it
referred to nothing concrete, because it refused to admit
its situation; it destroyed nothing because it rejected everything. But the black poet brings to surrealism his assumed
situation, in the intentional guise of condensed and concentrated obsessions; black poetry is "functional," that is,
responsive to a need that gives it exact definition. Aimé
Césaire destroys a very precisely defined culture; he ex-

presses very particular desires, though more than personal ones; and that which "he touches in the depths of his being is not the soul, it is a certain concrete and well determined form of humanity" (37). Here Sartre feels he can speak of an engaged and even directed mode of surrealist automatic writing, "not that there is the intervention of reflection, but because the words and the images continually express the same torrid obsession . . . the fixed inflexibility of vindication and of resentment" (37).

Where the European poets fail, as Sartre sees it, to fill out their poetry with meaningful and effective political sub-stance, Césaire creates a form of political poetry that is at once destructive, free, and "metaphysical." In doing so, he has also turned Sartre's conception of poetry on its head. In "Orphée noir" Sartre demonstrates that Césaire's poetry is *committed* poetry; despite the arguments of *Qu'est-ce que la littérature?* that poetry is not a form of committed literature, black poetry is, in our times, the "sole great revolutionary poetry" (11). So Césaire's poetry does ex-actly what poetry supposedly should not do: it changes the world. Césaire has managed to give situational, social, and political import to his poetry; his language is a tool, it has a function, and yet he continues to write in the poetic attitude. "That which tears itself from Césaire as a cry of grief, of love and of hate, is the *negritude-object*. Here, further, he follows the surrealist tradition which desires that the poem *objectivize*. The words of Césaire do not describe negritude, they do not designate it, they do not copy it from outside as a painter does of a model; they *make* it; they compose it under our eyes: henceforth it is a thing which one can observe and learn" (39).

In the context of our present argument, one can see that throughout these radical changes in Sartre's understanding of literature, despite the corresponding shifts in connecting

links in his broader theories, there remains constant in his
writing to this point the presence and development of the
dialectical network of personal myth that we discerned
underlying the earlier essays. The network was contradictory and nonlogical to begin with; in "Orphée noir" its
elements are sustained, but undergo a certain amount of
transformation, while its import and function remain the
same. Sartre uses his intuitions, and generalized half-truths
therefrom, to justify and support his arguments.

When the black poet triumphs where the European has
failed, one notes that in Sartre's mythology the black has
also supplanted the silent masculine peasant, at one with
nature, of "Aller et retour." "The black is first of all a
peasant. . . . Techniques have contaminated the white
worker, but the black remains the great male of the earth,
the sperm of the world. His existence—a great vegetal
patience; his work—the repetition from year to year of the
sacred coitus. He creates and is nourished because he
creates. . . . To labor, to plant, to eat, is to make love
with Nature" (44-45).

The contaminated white peasant no longer carries
mythological signficance for Sartre. The white peasant has
been betrayed by his culture, and the European has betrayed himself, by destroying his union with nature, his
humanity, and his masculinity. "The majority of the
images of the white poets tend toward a mineralization of
the human. Césaire, to the contrary, vegetalizes, animalizes
sea and sky and stone . . . the black stands witness to
the natural Eros; he manifests it and incarnates it; if one
wishes to find a term of comparison in European poetry,
he must return to Lucretius, the peasant poet who celebrated Venus, the mother god, in the times when Rome
was not yet much more than a great agricultural market. In
our day, I see only Lawrence to have had a cosmic sense of

sexuality. And, further, this sense in him remains extremely literary" (48).

From this first transformation, born in the idea that black poetry is an "agricultural" poetry, the whole complex of Sartrian heroism is transferred to the black poet. As the peasant stood in contrast to the bavard de salon, so the black poet's nature is understood in contrast to the flaccid asexuality of literary Europe, and so the black poet will incorporate masculinity, silence, and original unbetrayed unity with nature. According to Sartre, the black is at one with nature. At the same time, he is at one with all black humanity, for his most lyric, greatest poetry reaches surely toward collectivity beyond the individual, and he is at one with himself and his origins. He thinks not analytically or rationally, but by primitive, instinctive, rhythmic forms of synthetic sympathy with nature and Eros. Sartre sees negritude, in part, as an intuitive, sympathetic comprehension of human reality. In comparison with the European, the black seems more essential; "the sources of his existence and the roots of Being are identical" (44). "Being is black, Being is of fire, we are accidental and remote; we have to justify for ourselves our customs, our techniques, our 'undercooked' paleness, our verdigris vegetation" (10).

So the black poet can take on the heroic tasks of literature; he will be half prophet, half partisan, a "maker." He is Black Orpheus, plunging into himself, penetrating into nature to recapture his existential unity and original purity by "a progressive ascesis beyond the universe of discourse." He can reach back for his soul more successfully through language than Parain could reach back to an infrasilence or Bataille to a unity that existed before language, because "the black is closer than we to the great epoch in which, as Mallarmé says, 'the word creates the Gods'" (33).

The black poet lives in his own particular form of solitude: he is an exile, doubly separated from his original
land and from the depths of his soul. His untiring descent
to the "bursting hell" of the black soul shapes itself
through language, through the analytic forms of the
French language in particular ("that pale, cold language of
gooseflesh" [22]). Because this language separates what he
wants to say from what he says, as soon as he speaks of
himself, because he experiences the inevitable failure of
language, because the white oppressor is present in all
facets of this language, the black poet will speak French
only to destroy it. He will use the violent methods of surrealism to break the language into pieces and then build
from its ruins "a solemn and sacred superlanguage: Poetry"
(26). In many senses, this superlanguage replaces the infrasilence the white peasant sought, for it is itself a form of
silence, a captation of the world through magical stillness:
"Negritude is silence . . . short circuits of speech—and
there behind the flaming fall of words we perceive a huge
idol, black and mute" (27).

   In coming to the idea that negritude is silence, Sartre
allows us to see that he has not rejected the importance of
the paradoxical relationships between language and silence.
In "Orphée noir" he gives us one of his clearest exposi-
tions of the problem:

> . . . it is common knowledge that this feeling of
> failure before language when considered as a means
> of direct expression is at the source of all poetic
> experience.
>   The reaction of the *speaker* before this failure of
> prose is in effect that which Bataille names the holo-
> caust of words. Insofar as we can believe that a pre-
> established harmony rules the correspondence of the

Word and of Being, we employ words without seeing them, with a blind confidence. They are like sensory organs, like the mouth and the hands, open windows to the world. Upon the first failure, this babel falls outside of us; we see the system in its entirety, it is no more than an upset and deranged mechanism whose great arms still gesture grotesquely in space. We see immediately the folly of the enterprise of speech. We understand that language is, in essence, prose; and prose, in essence, failure. Being raises itself before us a tower of silence, and if we still wish to capture it, it can only be through silence, "to evoke, in a purposeful shadow the silent object by words always allusive, never direct, reducing themselves to a necessary equal silence." No one has more ably said that poetry is a necromantic attempt to induce being in and by the vibratory disappearance of the word. In improving upon his verbal impotence, in rendering words mad, the poet makes us suspect that beyond this clamor which cancels itself by itself, there are enormous densities of silence; and since we cannot silence ourselves, it is necessary to create a silence with language. From Mallarmé to the Surrealists, the profound aim of French poetry appears to me to have been this auto-destruction of the language. [24–25]

Although this analysis does not directly contradict Sartre's view of poets in *Qu'est-ce que la littérature?*, Sartre's attitude towards the poet seems to have modified itself, under the influence of Mallarmé. No longer is the poet accused of withdrawing the reader from the human condition and forcing him into the position of God, no longer is the privileged condition of prose as crucial as it was in *Qu'est-ce que la littérature?*, and no longer does the destruction of

language mean the collapse of only one of the many structures sustaining man. Sartre has discovered that the poet,
too, can change the world, that poetry can be an instrument and an arm, and that the poet's quasisilence, the
supersilence of negritude, can be an act.

The constructive, revolutionary potency of black poetry
is transposed by Sartre into his metaphorical scheme of
sexuality. In comparison with effeminate European littérateurs, the black is the male of the earth, the sperm of
nature. He sows his seed on a fecund, receptive terrain, his
labor and his poetry are carnal enjoyments of nature. But
in black poetry Sartre comes to see beyond the limits of
his obsession with masculine potency, for the cosmic
sexuality he finds in it, and to which he immediately re-
sponds, causes him to reevaluate the feminine element in
creativity. Within the bounds of "Orphée noir" the feminine elements of art (receptivity, patience, charm, rhythm)
are given almost equal value with masculine explosive
creativity. For the black poets

> being comes from non-being as a rising phallus. Crea-
> tion is an enormous and perpetual coition; the world is
> flesh and son of the flesh. On the sea and in the sky,
> on the sands, on the rocks, in the wind, the Negro re-
> discovers the velvetness of the human skin; he is "flesh
> of the flesh of the world"; he is "porous to its every
> breath," to all its pollen. He is by turn the female of
> Nature and its male; and when he makes love with a
> woman of his race, the sex act seems to him the cele-
> bration of the Mystery of being. This spermatic religion
> is like a tension of the soul balancing two complemen-
> tary tendencies; the dynamic emotion of being a rising
> phallus, and that softer, more patient and feminine, of

being a plant which grows. Thus negritude, in its most
profound origin, is androgyny. [47]

The androgynous nature of negritude coincides with the
twin techniques of black poetry that Sartre discusses. The
black poet seeks to return to his origins by two convergent
routes, one "objective," the other "subjective." In this
categorization of poetic techniques we may discern the
germs of the classification of imagination into masculine
and feminine types that we shall see Sartre developing in
Saint Genet.

In the objective search for the soul of his people, using
the objective poetic technique, "the poet as a spiritual
exercise submits himself to the fascination of primitive
rhythms, and allows his thought to run in the traditional
forms of black poetry. . . . The poetic act is then a
dance of the soul; the poet turns like a dervish until he ex-
pires, he has installed in himself the times of his ancestors,
he feels himself to flow away in spasmodic pulsations, and
it is in this rhythmic flowing away that he seeks to cause
himself to be possessed by the negritude of his people"
(31-33). Poetry here becomes the incantation of negritude,
as a form of magic or charm. And Sartre's objective poet,
possessed by his people, submitting—as we shall see Flaubert submit—to the power installed with him, is very much
a feminine poet. His poetic genius stems from rhythmic
receptivity; his labor is a passive patience (as Flaubert's
labor will be a *peine*); his synthesis, like that of Proust in
Saint Genet, is an inclusive, infolding, "retractile" embrace
and a horizontal, melting flow, an absorption of life and a
dissolution through sexual sympathy into life.

The subjective poet, whom Sartre still prefers, is, in contrast, an explosive male: his labor is a powerful vertical

descent and an inflexible erection, his genius a torrid obsession, his synthesis a tortured excretion and a fiery ejaculation. Aimé Césaire, as the subjective poet, descends in his poetry "beneath words and meanings," beneath the "first reefs of revolt," to "touch his feet finally in the black water of dreams and of desire, and to let himself drown in it. Then desire and dream will surge forth in a tidal roar, making words dance like wreckage, and will hurl them shattered on the shore" (33). Césaire, using the "old surrealist method," plunging into "the boiling bosom of Nature" and under the "superficial crust of reality," touching the basic desires that define man as negation, is able to revolutionize surrealism precisely because of the intense power of his poetry, generated by the fire of obsession, that is, his commitment to his situation. Surrealism in its European context failed in its revolutionary goals because its methods failed to raise its poetry above pseudo-objectivity and impersonality and because its poetry remained precious and gratuitous; but a poem by Aimé Césaire "bursts and turns on itself as a rocket, as bursting suns which turn and explode in new suns, in a perpetual surpassing. It is not a question of meeting in a calm unity of opposites but rather an almost sexual erection of one member of the couple 'black-white' in its opposition to the other. The density of these words, hurled into the air like rocks by a volcano, is negritude as it defines itself against Europe and colonisation" (36). Césaire's poetry erupts into synthesis and collectivity, and the collectivity of black poetry spirals off and into creative subjectivity. Black poetry can be revolutionary because, unlike other poetry, it unites subjectivity and objectivity in one huge totalizing act.

3

Saint Genet

Tantôt c'est un styliste qui, comme dit Gide, "se préfère"
et d'autres fois, tout simplement, c'est un grand écrivain.
Saint Genet

Jean Genet, abandoned child, thief, homosexual, prosti-
tute, traitor, and writer, serves as the subject of the central
work in Sartre's critical writing. Published in 1952, *Saint
Genet, Comédien et martyr,* the most brilliant and complex of Sartre's studies of writers, nonetheless fits the most
tightly into his system. As a more developed form of
existential psychoanalysis, it corrects the "insufficiencies"
Sartre perceived in *Baudelaire,* and it serves as a conduit to
his later thought at a time when Sartre was still discovering
Marxism. "I have tried to do the following: to indicate the
limit of psychoanalytic interpretation and Marxist explanation and to demonstrate that freedom alone can account
for a person in his totality; to show this freedom at grips
with destiny, crushed at first by its mischances, then turning upon them and digesting them little by little; to prove
that genius is not a gift but the way out that one invents in
desperate cases; to learn the choice that a writer makes of
himself, of his life and of the meaning of the universe, in-
cluding even the formal characteristics of his style and
composition, even the structure of his images and of the

particularity of his tastes; to review in detail the history of his liberation" (536).[1]

In *Saint Genet* Sartre clearly distinguishes between masculine and feminine types of imagination. In opposing what he calls the "humanistic" universe of Rimbaud and Nietzsche, where the forces of negation explode all conceivable limits (504), to the stable and "theological" universe of Genet, Baudelaire, and Mallarmé, "in which a divine crosier shepherds things together in flocks, imposing unity upon discontinuity itself" (504), Sartre writes, "This perhaps parallels a distinction between the 'feminine' imagination (which reinforces in the woman—when she is her master's accomplice—the illusion of being at the center of a beautiful order [*un beau cosmos tout fait*]) and the 'virile' explosive imagination (which contains and transcends anguish by means of the images it forms)" (505).[2] As we have noted, the specificity of feminine imagination is not limited to women alone but rather constitutes an ontological possibility open to each human liberty. As Sartre made clear in *Baudelaire,* femininity is a way of looking at and perceiving the world—a choice of values, tastes, and perceptions. It is not a question of biological status, but of social condition(ing) and choice. Sartre can therefore lead us from this first distinction to a subsequent classification of all writers into masculine and feminine camps, as long as we remember that for him Mallarmé and Rimbaud represent two pure and opposed types of imagi-

---

1. Page references that follow in the text are to the translation by Bernard Frechtman.

2. The feminine imagination embodies an "illusion" here, while the masculine imagination embodies an act of transcendence, so we rejoin and clarify the two possibilities offered for imagination in *L'Imaginaire.* Literature is condemned, in one sense, to operate an act of irrealization, both of writer and reader, but in Genet we shall see the potential value of such an act.

nation and that between them lies an entire transitional series of mixed types.

Sartre measures Rimbaud and Genet in terms of this opposition. Rimbaud's explosive images give proof of a "virile generosity"; they are "ejaculations" bespeaking an undertaking, a projection toward the future through action that will "unify the diverse." But Genet's passivity seats him at the center of a predetermined world. "Incapable of *carving out* a place for himself in the universe, he *imagines* in order to convince himself that he created the world that excludes him" (505). Genet does not choose to imagine heroically in order to force the world to submit to him, but because reality defeats him.

The masculine and feminine imaginations take shape in modern literature, Sartre holds, in two corresponding types of poetic unification, one "expansive," the other "retractile." In both cases, the work of the artist is to offer glimpses of an aesthetic order lying behind the whims of chance (which might imply an incorrigible inauthenticity in all forms of art). Expansive unification accompanies the masculine imagination; it creates the world of Nietzsche and Rimbaud:

> But the first tendency—which is that of Rimbaud—forcibly compels a natural diversity to symbolize an *explosive unity.* We are gradually made to see in a miscellaneous collection the breaking up of a prior totality whose elements, set in motion by a centrifugal force, break away from each other and fly off into space, colonizing it and there reconstituting a new unity. To see the dawn as a "people of doves" is to blow up the morning as if it were a powder keg. Far from denying plurality, one discovers it everywhere, one exaggerates it, but only to present it as a moment in a progression;

it is the abstract instant that congeals it into an exploding but static beauty. Impenetrability, which is an inert resistance of space, the sagging of a dead weight, is transformed into a conquering force, and infinite divisibility into a glorious burst of continuity; persons are refulgent sprays whose dynamic unity is combustion. If this violence congeals, the flare falls in a rain of ashes. We shall *then* have discontinuity and number, those two names of death. But as long as the explosion lasts, juxtaposition signifies progress. *Beside* means *beyond.* For each object, scattered everywhere, in all directions, launched with all the others upon an infinite course, to *be* is to participate in the raging tide whereby the universe at every moment wins new areas of being from nothingness. This Dionysian imagery gladdens our hearts, fills us with a sense of power. It derives its force from an imperial pride, from a generosity that gushes forth and spends itself utterly. Its aim is to force the externality of Nature to reflect back to man his own transcendence. For those who want "to change life," "to reinvent love," God is nothing but a hindrance. If the unity is not dynamic, if it manifests itself in the form of restrictive contours, it reflects the image of their chains. Revolutionaries break the shells of being; the yolk flows everywhere. [500]

In comparison with revolutionary poets, Genet, Mallarmé, and Proust seem "miserly." According to Sartre's severe and simplistic interpretation (which here ignores the true dynamism of all three), their poetic unification is retractile, their feminine imaginations squeeze together a girdled and tamed universe. "Proust, too, has a tendency to tighten the bonds of the real world, which are always a little loose, to give an additional turn of the screw, to assume that there is an order among objects that actually have none. The author of *Cities of the Plains,* also a homosexual and a recluse, likewise practiced 'a selection among things which rids [him] of their usual appearance and enables [him] to perceive analogies'" (502). The feminine imagination imposes stability on a disordered world without transcending that disorder, primarily through the illusory devices of analogy and identification (the assumption of deep identity behind apparent similarity and of common qualities in distinct entities; the idea that things "are what they are"), that is, through what Sartre considers the false supposition of coherence.[3]

The distinction between the two forms of poetic technique in *Saint Genet* develops immediately from the discussion of subjective and objective techniques in "Orphée noir." In a similar fashion the classification of masculine and feminine imaginations had its birth in the dichotomies outlined in the essay on Husserl. The feminine poet is a Penelope gathering home the sailor and a spider-fisherman pulling in the nets—the "spider-spirit" of idealism, who drew all things into its net and reduced them to its own substance. As opposed to the existentialist vision of a

3. Since analogy and identification are commonly considered primary devices of symbolism, it should be clear to what extent Sartre's views are oriented toward a rejection of the symbolist tradition—in the principle of universal analogy inherited from Baudelaire, most precisely—and the symbolist fathers (no matter how feminine they have become here). It is hardly original to point out that Sartre's criticism can be seen from an overview as an assassination of the (literary) father (Proust and Flaubert are the masters behind *La Nausée; L'Etre et le Néant* is written against Freud, etc.) and Sartre's biographers have linked this to his antipathy for the nineteenth-century heroes (Bourget, Barrès) of his grandfather, ersatz father. Sartre's quest, then, would be for the misplaced real father, who seems to live in either eighteenth-century France or twentieth-century Germany. Balancing this tendency is the struggle with his surrealist contemporaries, and their replacement by more authentic— if temporary—brothers: Camus, Dos Passos, Nizan.

novelist who would respect the "freedom" of his characters, Genet's imagination is "essentialist"; he shares with
Proust the same "fundamental resentment, the same contemplative quietism, the same Platonism" (503). Like the
objective poetic technique of "Orphée noir," retractile
unification operates by magic or charm, patience, and a
flow of opposites and discontinuity into unity through
analogy; it operates, as did idealism, by assimilation,
identification, and unification—by digestion. The Eternal
Feminine here is an onflowing river, a principle of erosion.
Similarly, expansive unification embodies the major
elements of subjective poetry as a "virile generosity" that
seeks to transcend disorder and disunity without denying
them.

    In "Orphée noir" and in the essay on intentionality, it
was clear that Sartre found greater potential in the subjective form of poetry and was more drawn to the masculine
mode of existence. Césaire, the subjective poet, weighed
far heavier in the balance than Etienne Léro, his precursor.
Léro's exploitation of surrealism created poems that
remained closed upon themselves, that were nothing more
than imitations and student exercises, while Césaire revolutionized all of surrealism and poetry. The Husserlian hero
surpassed his weak-kneed, protected predecessor; Jean-Paul,
as the imitation hero-writer of *Les Mots,* had at least
greater potential for explosive self-liberation than did the
false child he once was. The line of preference was even
reinforced in terms of clear political distinctions: the
effeminate European oppressor of "Orphée noir" was
clearly less capable of authentic creation, less worthy of
our regard, than his fiery black victim. In *Saint Genet*
Sartre hints coyly at the same idea: "If I were not afraid
of opening the way to excessive simplification and of being
misunderstood, I would say that there is a 'leftist' turn of

imagination and a 'rightist' one. The former aims at representing the unity that human labor forcibly imposes upon the disparate; the latter, at depicting the entire world in accordance with the type of a hierarchical society" (500). We may easily guess that Sartre's preference would hardly go to the "rightist" style, which he makes analogous to the feminine imagination.

But in *Saint Genet* Sartre's tastes and preferences are no longer so clearly marked as they were before "Orphée noir." Although masculinity is still associated with generosity, liberty, pride, force, and heroism, Sartre's argument no longer drips with horror of the feminine; his cosmic sexuality is less frightened, more tempered, more tolerant. In "Orphée noir" we observed a movement towards a wider vision of creativity; the encounter with Genet has changed Sartre's views still more.

Originally Genet's imagination is of the feminine type; his sensitivity is naive, fresh, "folkloric," and girlish. A little "hoodlum with delicate tastes," entrances by facile poetry and illusory glitter, he dreams the dreams of a shop-girl. The form of his imagination is both a product of his constituted feminine passivity and a choice; as an outcast Genet needs evil to affirm the prior existence of good and order. Genet chooses to affirm the magic indivisibility and unity of the universe, he chooses to envisage a prepackaged world, where the principle of cohesion conquers all disintegration. His choice is of a mode of being, a project, that Sartre defines as feminine, for the essence of the feminine imagination centers on the illusion of being at the heart of a "beau cosmos tout fait." Genet makes of his hierarchical and egocentric world view the principle of his art, and it is precisely the classic rigor of unity of this vision that Sartre sees as the source of the "singular beauty" of Genet's work.[4]

4. Here Sartre uses the concept of classicism in a different sense from the

The only rule of composition in Genet's writing is Genet himself, for he himself is the single internal structure of his work. "He has put all of himself into his work; his book is himself . . . to compose, for him, is to recreate himself" (584). In most of Genet's descriptions, Sartre says, a circular movement organizes itself, and the objects described turn in towards an immobile center. That center is Genet himself.

The technique of Genet's unification is naturally retractile. At every moment, "his patient will-to-unify is constricting, confining; it is always marking out limits and grouping things together. . . . Genet's image, instead of bringing the flowers *out* of the branch, brings them *back* to it, glues them to the wood. The movement of the image is from without inward, from the wings to the axis. In general, his poetic patterns present closed and stable units" (500–01). In comparison with the Dionysian terrorism of the surrealists, Genet is for Sartre a "rhetorician," a puritan of style, an ascetic of restraint. Genet's art is feminine; its intention is seduction: "His literary adventure [*sa tentative littéraire*] is not unlike an amorous adventure: while seeking to arouse horror, Genet writes in order to be loved" (591). Genet flirts with the reader, offers himself, and lets himself be taken: "Coquetry, finery, masochism: such are the mainsprings of Genet's art, an art feminine in its nature" (592). Despite certain resemblances between Genet and Rimbaud (and the surrealists), despite Genet's potential for explosive self-multiplication, Sartre places early Genet squarely in the line he has established of the overly maternalized Baudelaire, of discreet, feminine Mallarmé, and of Proust, homosexual and recluse.

---

one he used in relation to Camus earlier. But Camus, too, insisted on the spirit of unity (interiority) rather than totality (exterior) as the principle of art. (*L'Homme révolté*.)

What we have obviously left out of consideration to this point is the most salient fact about Genet: he is a homosexual. Sartre's conclusions about masculine and feminine imaginations, his demonstration of the retractile nature of Genet's art, develop out of the thought that "there is a certain pederastic and criminal twist to his imagination" (499). If Sartre's views have undergone modification in *Saint Genet*, one reason is that in the encounter with Genet, Sartre faces the feminine menace to masculinity in its most specific and most immediate form. He is able in *Saint Genet* to deal with homosexuality directly (if abstractly) and perhaps to put into balance its hypothetically personal threat to him; at the least, he accords to Genet a sympathy he has always denied Proust. Of course, in the case of Genet, what he says is heavily clothed in moral self-righteousness: where Proustian homosexuality apparently offers only an overly refined and guiltily bourgeois distillation of idealist mechanics, an imperialistic ingestion of the world into a homosexual paste, Genet's inversion approaches willfully the limit points of negativity; it is an instrument and a weapon against bourgeois society. Sartre can accept homosexuality in Genet, must accept it; one might surmise that this acceptance allows him to become less afraid for himself, more confident in his own virility. He himself, he tells the reader, has no particular taste for young boys and no police record, yet Genet's writings have moved him. *Nous voilà délivrés de Proust,* as Sartre becomes Genet's apologist: "Where's the crime? Where's the enormity? Human relations are possible between homosexuals just as between a man and a woman. Homosexuals can love, give, elevate each other and elevate themselves" (248).

Sartre both stresses and undercuts the discrete import of Genet's homosexuality. He at once pinpoints the specifically homosexual nature of Genet's writings with surprising precision and at the same time reduces it to a mere mode of feminine passivity among others.

First, Genet's homosexuality lies at the root of his art, at the source of his images and his language. Homosexuality, like all human relationships, comprises an attempt to communicate. As Sartre sees it, the passive homosexual speaks to take revenge on the world, and his tools are analysis and myth. Genet and Proust, then, both have "wicked souls, that is, souls which are solitary and tender, fabulous and corrosive" (150); they share a "pederastic malice" that metamorphoses men into symbolic, frozen objects. Central to Genet's art is a tremendous will to shape reality into a unified social hierarchy, from which he is excluded as criminal and homosexual. The feudal and monarchical society that he dreamed of as an adolescent he transmutes, through analogy and sacramental assimilation, into his imaginary reality. He names to transform, to invert.

Such is the general impetus that shapes Genet's art, but beyond this Sartre traces the exact influence of homosexuality to a point of precision that seems dubious. What one might accept in Sartre as novelist, when in *Les Chemins de la liberté* he invests Daniel Sereno with a "long, pederastic patience," may be harder to justify in Sartre's criticism. In considering Genet's phrase, "The gardener is the loveliest rose in his garden," Sartre declares, "A homosexual sentence if ever there was one, and more so in its form than its content" (548). Without the necessity of referring to context, this sentence, Sartre decrees, is homosexual in essence. His justification is both theoretical and concrete. Since all literature expresses the totality of its author, and each of Genet's creative acts "realizes a totalization," since the phrase itself establishes a "short-circuit" between a banal and sensible image and an unrealizable sense, since the proposition offers itself and denies itself to the reader at the same time, Sartre discerns in both form and content that particular form of betrayal that he defines as homosexuality. We thus have an explicit vision of homosexuality and a direct application of that vision, but we are offered no directions on further usage of the tool that has been given us. Are all of Genet's uses of language to be considered implicitly homosexual? Are there any that escape such a judgment? Is there nothing in this image but perversion? And are all uses of language that destroy language to be considered homosexual?[5]

Although he has given homosexuality a clear frame of reference, having assimilated it to betrayal, Sartre has also made it very general. Betrayal and homosexuality are subsumed to metaphysical principles, evil and femininity; Genet's sexuality is only the force of evil realized in flesh. Homosexuality is but a subordinate form of femininity, of relative being.

In Genet's strict opposition of the "dur" and the "mou," the tough and the fairy, the active and the passive pederast, in the master-slave relationship of *l'amant* and *l'aimé*, there exist visible parallels to Sartre's own intuitive world view. In this light Genet's homosexuality would be considered essentially feminine only as long as he remains the passive partner.[6] And when Genet does change his role in the course of time, he seems indeed to acquire a measure of virility. But Sartre points out that in this role change Genet relearns his character Mignon's discovery, "A male who fucks another male is not a double male; he is a fairy"

5. The surrealist image, frequently self-destructive, always questioning language as language, would then be homosexual in form and content. So, too, would many forms of humor.

6. The active partner in Genet's system is beloved and indifferent; the passive partner is the unrequited lover, used as a convenient object in the sexual act.

(443). In reality, Genet is never more than a "false male," his virility remains entirely imaginary, his sexuality entirely perverted: his passive homosexuality is his "secret." A homosexual may aspire to anything but virility, for homosexuality at base is feminine submission.

In addition, as more than one critic has noticed, Sartre directly denies the importance of any actual physical pleasure that Genet may experience in homosexual activity. Though pleasure becomes an element when Genet takes the role of the active partner, it is accidental and inappropriate. Genet's sexual experiences are acts of revenge on the bourgeoisie, of submission to rape by the Other, of abjection, of symbolic gesture and magical ceremony. His sexuality is an empty game, a false front; it is a refusal of or an indifference to orgasm; it includes no abandon, no loss of self: it is suffering, rage, and humiliation whose immediate controlled end is the pleasure of the Other. (In the homosexual act the passive partner becomes "a female and contemptible object . . . a receptacle, a vase, a spittoon" [125].) Genet recreates over and over his original crisis, the verbal rape of Genet the child, and the reality of any sexual act appears to nullify itself in favor of its eternal meaning.

What Sartre has done is to negate the specific experience of homosexual activity—or, rather, by minimizing its most present and perhaps most important motivation, physical pleasure, he has made it almost cosmically determined. Genet's homosexuality is defined by Sartre primarily in terms of social relationships, and each physical act can be associated to metaphysical principles. Genet's sexuality appears not to have been born in any attraction to males but is rather a result of his relative being; his motivation in the sexual act is the search for being under the feminine impulse. Even his femininity is evanescent, an absence, a *pis-aller,* a pure contestation of virility; men make the law, and women and Genet are the victims. In the same way that he chooses the imaginary (again a pis-aller) because he cannot "carve himself a place in the universe," similarly, "since he is denied the right to be a man, he will make himself into a woman" (320).

A number of issues important to us are involved in Sartre's understanding of Genet's imagination. The most crucial of them appear when Sartre extends his perception of the precise nature of Genet's (criminal and homosexual) imagination to the idea that there exists an authentic, primitive form of imagination and literary style that we may recognize as specific to Genet, and that there is also possible a secondary level of imagination and style that is not authentic Genet. For example, Genet may use the surrealist explosive-subjective method in writing, but in Sartre's estimation it is not natural to him. In Genet's writings Sartre will claim the right to distinguish between authentic Genet and false Genet.

Sartre justifies his discrimination between authentic and impure Genet styles along the lines of his general understanding of Genet's history. He deems certain of Genet's utterances and certain lines of his poetry authentic and complete because they are each recreations and negations of Genet's original crisis and because they emerge directly from Genet's relationship to language.

As an adolescent, Genet lives as an exile from language. The nonadaptation toward language that Parain, Ponge, and Bataille felt intermittently, the estrangement from words in their socialized context of prose, becomes constant and radical in Genet. Each of the others returns to his job as editor, librarian, or salesman, while Genet remains apart. As a child ostracized from the bourgeois society of the just, condemned as a thief, objectified by a name, he realizes that the socialization of language, the changing of language from a natural phenomenon into a tool, makes language work against him. He is crystallized for others, branded by the word "thief." He is produced synthetically by language, by a freezing process that makes of him "the thief," a butterfly pierced through by a word, and from that moment he loses the use of words, except by chance, or as he steals them, too. "Genet was condemned to silence: a culprit does not speak. . . . In the old days, they simply cut off a delinquent's tongue; our society, which is more humane, lets him keep his organs of phonation on condition that he not use them" (304).

Since society forbids Genet all *use* of language, the only possible relationship to language left him is poetic.

> Moreover, let him use *words* as much as he likes: Society has put *things* in safekeeping. The vocables which he learns refer to forbidden realities. . . . Our words turn their backs to him, designate absences, denote distances, name invisible things, refer to what is manifest to others and remains hidden from his eyes: they are repositories of unrealizable intuitions. No doubt he understands the "socialized" meaning of the vocables he uses, but this meaning remains abstract. No doubt he can assemble them to make sentences, but he does so like a blind man. . . . He speaks: this means that words pop up out there in society and assemble and take on all by themselves a meaning that escapes him. [305]

Society has stripped away all signification, all reference, from his words; he can have no normal relationship of prose or communication to language. Prose entails dialogue, reciprocity: how can Genet, the outcast, be but a poet or a mute? Since the significative use of language is forbidden, Genet's attention turns to what Sartre deems "nonsignifying" language, the magic discourse of poetry. Language can be for Genet neither natural nor utilitarian; it can only be miraculous. "In our rapid, condensed, scraggy, hacked soliloquies, words pass unnoticed, they serve as points of reference for our thoughts and gestures; in the case of Genet, the constant displacement which separates them from what they name fixes his attention on them. . . . words, in him, are like foreign bodies; he observes them, examines, runs them in neutral, just to see. As the designated objects are all equally taboo, myth and reality are equivalent" (306). As Genet was crystallized by a word, so he names not to signify, but to transform: "To change words is to change Being" (306). What counts for him is the material presence of the word. Certain words count for more, miraculously, and with their appearance his imagination begins to take shape.

Genet's separation from the normal usage of language, and the fact that a word has shaped him into an impulse toward negativity, feed back into a destruction of language. As Genet changes into a poet because he wants to make of himself a thief, he twists the language he is allowed to use, he isolates it, and watches it crack from below. The impetus towards negativity and Genet's exile from prose cause his language to function emptily and in a void, cause him to reverse the use of language, to turn communication into its opposite. Through systematic lying, through the continued perversion of the concept of communication, Genet uses language to destroy language.[7]

Since words have for him no instrumental value, since

7. Sartre offers the example of Genet "denying the evidence" when questioned by the police: a thief has been identified as having Genet's hair, clothes, face, fingerprints, and name. Genet's response: "It's not me" (p. 310).

Genet is confined to the role of passive auditor and not
allowed to speak, "language is isolated, in the manner of
the Latin of the Mass, it is the object of an aesthetic intuition: the play of the sonant volutes seems to obey a finality
without end" (315). Genet cannot for long consent to
remain silent (since language as being-for-others necessarily
demands his attention), but he no longer understands the
utility of words; when he speaks, then, he speaks to
destroy common prose through aesthetic intuition. He
chooses to utter certain words, because he feels intuitively
that they are miraculous and poetic, that in pronouncing
them he transforms the world. He destroys prose by
introducing poetry into it, by denying to it all reciprocity.
He utters a phrase; either he is lying, inverting meaning, or
the words may be true, but the speaker, Genet as false
bourgeois, false tough, or false woman, is imaginary. "The
words telescope, interfere, they burn and corrode each
other; as a result of the injury they do each other, their
meaning flies and is lost in the infinite. . . . Poems are
born in him like crimes, language turns away from its
original destination" (322, 336).

How does Genet know which words are miraculous,
which words are poetry that will destroy prose? How does
he recognize a "sacred," "prestigious," "vertiginous"
word?

> Answer: by the poetic emotion it arouses. And what is
> poetic emotion? Nothing other than the exorcising
> repetitions of the original crisis. One day, when he was
> caught pilfering, the word "thief" struck him like
> lightning, and the earth opened beneath his feet: he
> felt himself escaping and becoming a thief elsewhere,
> in the minds of others; a social and inaccessible order
> of language manifested itself. The poetic emotion

> surges up when he hears certain words uttered unex-
> pectedly, and this too is a dizziness. . . . It is the ver-
> tigo, the want, the nothingness, and the negation
> which mark the poetic emotion. A word strikes him,
> the ground opens up: the poem is born (there exist, for
> Genet, poems composed of a single word). [325–26]

Certain words swell up all at once in Genet's throat, an
anonymous voice whispers suddenly inside him, the world
spins, and Genet finds himself the author of a poem. The
aesthetic emotion he feels is a happy one, for Genet's
poetry operates as an antidote to his condemnation. A
poem is born in him when an unexpected word lets him
glimpse a hidden necessity in things, lets him sense intuitively an aesthetic order in language and in the universe, an
order in which he is not condemned but the only chosen
one of God, in which he himself is God, his own absent
witness, and "son propre élu":

> So Genet has become a poet. But let there be no
> misunderstanding: his poetry is not a literary art, it is a
> means of salvation. He does not write or recite his
> poems, which, moreover, are often reduced to a single
> word. Poetry does not issue forth from him, it is not
> intended for a public: it is a way of life. . . . And it
> is not an inner sweetness of words already understood
> that imparts to them their poetic value: quite the con-
> trary, they are glazed, varnished, stately, they are ad-
> dressed to another and flee Genet in the night of
> unknowing: "Allusive words reduced to equal silence,"
> like those of Mallarmé. [329–30]

It is the frozen necessity of the miraculous word in Genet
that allows Sartre to develop his claim for a primitive authenticity in parts of Genet's writing. From the prestigious

word evolve in the adolescent Genet fragments of poetry,
isolated lines that are solid things, monolithic blocks
welded together by affinities of sound and rhythm:

> Driven away everywhere, the young Cain roves
> about, in Spain, in Poland, in Czechoslovakia. He is
> twenty years old, twenty-two. He walks in silence. Yet
> at every breath words fill his mouth. They come all by
> themselves, as in dreams. The rhythm of his pace and
> breath gives rise to vague phrases which break beneath
> their own weight. To whom is he speaking? To nobody.
> No intention of designating, of communicating, of
> teaching. And who is speaking? Nobody. Or, rather,
> language itself . . .
> These phrases which assemble by themselves have
> the inertia of material figures. Genet listens to them,
> he observes without intervening. This passivity is partly
> feigned: it is he who utters the words. It is true that
> the rhythm of his pace determines his breathing, that
> he feels the beat even in his throat, that it creates
> verbal patterns, selects words; it is true that Genet does
> not think, that he is thought; it is true that by dint of
> repeating the words with which he enraptures himself
> he engenders, by virtue of assonance, alliteration and
> external similitude, units of sound composed of agglu-
> tinative words; it is true that he is sometimes surprised
> by these conglomerates. But this policy of noninter-
> vention is calculated: its aim is to capture the word.
> [330-31]

This, then, is the source and the form of authenticity in
Genet's writing: the frozen sacred word and the "bloc
sonore," ceremonial incantations, illogical and undifferentiated, intended to capture reality, spoken only to an

absent witness, that have no signification but an inert and bulky *sense,* that do not designate but *are.*

In the chapter "Un mécanisme ayant du vers l'exacte rigeur" Sartre studies Genet's first creative act, the act that makes of him a writer, that transforms a "little unfortunate thief" into Jean Genet: the poem Genet wrote in prison, "Le Condamné à mort."

> Le vent qui roule un coeur sur le pavé des cours
> Un ange qui sanglote accroché dans un arbre
> La colonne d'azur qu'entortille le marbre
> Font ouvrir dans ma nuit des portes de secours.

In the first and third lines of this first verse of the poem Sartre sees the original substrata of the quatrain and perhaps of the whole poem. Each of these lines represents a "bloc sonore," a cluster of sounds formed inside Genet involuntarily and without connection—authentic Genet, expressed in discontinuous poetic intuitions. Genet had heard them whispered in the back of his throat, months or years before, and he had submitted to them; they are whole, entire, mystically self-contained. "They had existed for a long time, hard, encysted, pure *things,* before Genet dreamed of uniting them" (468).

The second and fourth lines Sartre feels to be very different. The second line he terms a synthetic pearl, a chemical reconstitution. In it Genet has voluntarily attempted to reproduce the first and third lines, but he has not succeeded in imitating anything but exterior form. The line is not authentically personal; its vocabulary and its images are gratuitous, borrowed from other authors, from Baudelaire or Cocteau, for example, for neither angels nor archangels are part of his "accessories." For Sartre the line is insincere and facile; it makes bad, insipid, and counterfeit poetry.

While the theme of the fourth line represents authentic

Genet, it, too, is artificially conceived. As an explanation invented after the fact, the fourth line attempts to unify Genet's poetic intuitions into discursive sense. Here Genet transcribes, he translates, he works unsuccessfully to create a cohesive poem. "The 'poetised' poet who *experienced* his poems becomes a versifier who *makes* them" (395): he links together unattached entities "by a web of meanings, a conjunctive tissue . . . in short by *prosaisms*" (459). Logic supersedes poetic meaning. Though his verses may charm by their rude, primitive richness, "they are caught up in a kind of poetic jelly, in the quivering inconsistency of superimposed imaginary layers" (476).

Ripples of obsession trouble the surface of Sartre's tranquil analysis. We are obliged to recognize that Sartre has shaped his vision of authenticity in Genet, with willful lucidity or not, so that it echoes in feeling and reference the intuitive Sartrian dichotomies. The "blocs sonores" are hard, encysted things, rude, primitive and whole; Genet as versifier envelops them in a false poetic jelly that is really prose. Sartre's images recreated the sexual overtones of the essays on Parain and Renard, the dualistic universe of the male's silent poetic intuition, and the subsequent betrayal of communication. Elsewhere in *Saint Genet* Sartre opposes Genet's solitude to the presence of the Other, "that warm, diffused atmosphere which envelops us" (635). Once again the individual as hero is surrounded by an enclosing feminine society, and the hard, knifelike projection of intuition is smothered in the rubbery womb of universalized, socialized language. Sartre's metaphysical system opposes purity to impurity and the hard *netteté* that is masculinity to the viscous mixture of femininity; his understanding of authenticity in Genet must be seen in this light. On at least one level of his analysis, Sartre equates authenticity with purity and inauthenticity with adulteration. In addition, his previous identification of poetry with childish inauthenticity and prose with meaningful action will be seen to negate itself, which is something critics of Sartre's aesthetics do not understand as long as they ignore *Saint Genet* and subsequent works.

The reappearance of dualistic tendencies in Sartre's thought disturbs the uneasy balance of his simultaneously synthetic and analytic attempt to depict Genet's enterprise in its totality. If one only forces the argument a bit, one can almost make Sartre imply that, in the name of the unity of Genet's project and its inherent unresolved contradictions, its nondialectic dualisms, there exists in Genet an authentic style that excludes parts of his writing, a primitive form of imagination defined to preclude "adulterated" creative expression, a nature beyond the actualities of its expression, or perhaps even prior to action. One part of Genet is Genet, while another is not; there are elements in Genet foreign to Genet. This development, of course, pushes Sartre's analysis beyond its intention, as it makes of him an essentialist. Nonetheless, Sartre has backed himself into an uncomfortable position. Once Genet has used a certain image or a certain technique in his poetry, can Sartre really say that they are not natural to him, that they are not part of his "accessories"?

Genet's homosexuality and his criminality mark his imagination distinctly and express themselves in acts that Sartre deems authentic. Both homosexuality and criminality, however, are products of a free choice by Genet, as well as being results of his objectivization, that is, his feminization. In the terms of Sartre's analysis, Genet *becomes* a homosexual because he is a thief, because his original crisis constituted an act of rape, because his condemnation causes in him a general inversion that directs him towards the antinatural, the artificial, and the dead,

because he has been made an object. Even before his condemnation his situation is false, dependent; even before
society rejects him, he is made an object by his mother's
rejection, but it is the dizzying moment of the original
crisis that shapes his history. "Sexually, Genet is first of all
a raped child. This first rape was the gaze of the other,
who took him by surprise, penetrated him transforming
him forever into an object. Let there be no misunderstanding: I am not saying that his original crisis *resembles* a
rape. I say that it *is* one . . . Genet has now been de-
flowered; an iron embrace has made him a woman. All that
is left for him is to put up with *being*. He is the village
whore; everyone can have him at will. Undressed by the
eyes of the decent folk as women are by those of males, he
carries his fault as they do their breasts and behind" (92).
Genet has been made a thief, he has been made a woman,
and at the same time he chooses to be a thief and woman—
he is, to judge by the linguistic patterns of *Saint Genet,* a
past participle and a present tense: his acts are judged
authentic or not as they express this double postulate. And
the sole arbiter here is Sartre's categorization of the world,
which does not always depend on Genet; the explosive-
subjective method in poetry cannot be natural or sincere in
Genet because Sartre does not consider it feminine.

The sexual connotations of Genet's authenticity are but
reflections of the larger sexual interpretation Sartre offers
for Genet's entire history. Sartre's Genet can be understood on a sexual level simply by equating "object" with
"female" and "subject" with "male"; Genet's project is to
pursue to the end his condition: he will be the object, the
Other, evil, he will make himself into a woman. On the
basis of this interpretation, his developing relationship to
literature, his liberation through writing, can be understood
completely in terms of sexuality.

Originally, Genet writes to seduce, to offer himself, to make of himself an object of love and hate, to be manipulated and noticed. His art, as we have noted, is feminine. But, in the last of his metamorphoses, after his "demivirilization," the nature of his art begins to change, and his sexual role *as writer* reverses. He slowly discovers his readers, he rediscovers prose, and he eventually introduces reciprocity and the idea of dialogue into his writing. In writing he finds an escape from his condemnation, a liberation; he manages through a false prose that is an assassination and a perversion of literature, a trap for the reader, to deobjectify and to defeminize himself (within the realm of the imaginary):

> Consequently, it is the reader who assumes the contradictions of Genet, who, as we have just seen, was both the beloved—since he made himself a thing to be taken—and the lover—since he took upon himself all the sufferings of love. The reader is going to experience the conflict in reverse: he will become a *lover* by the act of reading, he will attempt to slip into the thief's subjectivity; he will become an inessential subject by losing himself so that the object, Jean Genet, a legendary thief, may be. But no sooner has he entered this foreign subjectivity than he feels that an ironic gaze is objectifying him, and becomes a *thing to be taken,* to be handled, like a beloved creature. Inversely, Genet, who offered himself to the readers as an object, suddenly transforms himself, as soon as they have opened the book, into a subject. [592-93]

Genet reinvents the male role of the writer, as he makes of his public the vast feminine receptivity, the "immense feminine questioning," portrayed in *Qu'est-ce que la littérature?*. "The readers are being tricked: they are damning

themselves and some demiurge is watching them damn
themselves. A cynical and peremptory freedom is imposing
itself on their freedom, is enveloping it and maneuvering
it. . . . Bending over his paralyzed victims . . . he is a
gaze that rises up from the word . . . he has been crowned
king by the reader . . . his audience humbles itself before
him . . . he screws us: that is the consecration of the Poet"
(593-94). His art develops a masculine projection: "[The
pimps] were silent, implacable, steeped in indifference:
such is his work. Darling cleft the girl queens in two slices
which came together again with sigh: this sickle stroke,
this path of a cold, gleaming blade which one thinks one
possesses and which slides without leaving a trace is the
passing of one of Genet's poems through our mind" (592).
The art that Roquentin dreamed of, "beautiful and hard as
steel," has become Genet's.

From the image of the poet and the reader coupled in
the sexual act, from Genet's rape of the other's liberty,
Sartre makes a surprising extension:

> "I will be the Thief," says Genet. And now: "I am *the*
> Poet." With regard to this privileged case, we shall note
> one of the essential differences that set the poet off
> from the writer of prose. The latter, who is *profane* by
> nature, recognizes his readers' freedom exactly insofar
> as he asks them to recognize his: prose is based on this
> reciprocity of recognition. The poet, on the other
> hand, requires that he be recognized by a public which
> he does not recognize. The writer of prose *speaks* to
> the reader, attempts to convince him in order to
> achieve unanimous agreement on one point or other;
> the poet speaks to himself through the mediation of
> the reader. The writer of prose uses language as a
> middle term between himself and the Other; the poet

makes use of the Other as an intermediary between
language and himself. Between the writer of prose and
the reader, language is canceled so as to further the
ideas of which it has been the vehicle; between language and the poet, it is the reader who tends to be
effaced in order to become a pure vehicle of the poem;
his role is *to objectify speech* in order to reflect to the
poet his creative subjectivity in the form of sacred
power. [594-95]

We have noticed in "Orphée noir" and *Saint Genet*
modifications in Sartre's opinions about the latent creative
powers of femininity; we must now recognize the conclusion of a similar development in his understanding of
poetry. Aimé Césaire revolutionized poetry for Sartre; his
"torrid obsession," his commitment, his direction of the
surrealist technique, gave to poetry a massive masculine
impulse. The results of this new attitude can be found in
Sartre's discussions of prose and poetry in *Saint Genet,*
where the values of poetry and prose begin to coincide.

Genet's prose serves only as "the means of his poetry."
"If poetry is assassination, it must be given something to
assassinate; and if crime is a systematic destruction of
order, there must first have been the most vigorous order"
(543). His poetry "devours" his prose; "a dizzying flight
from signification to nothingness" (554), it punches holes
and lays traps everywhere in his elegant rhetoric. In describing Genet's will to poetry, Sartre conveys the feeling
of great strength, an intense, masculine, heroic effort to
keep free of the tepid flow of dialogue: "Genet debout,
raide, hérissé s'applique à tenir la tête hors de l'eau"
(Genet remains standing, stiff, bristling, determined to keep
his head above water [552]). By the end of *Saint Genet*
poetry has acquired a forcefully masculine connotation for

Sartre. The image of poetry approaches that of rape: the rape of the reader's liberty, which the poet does not recognize.[8] The reader becomes a mere vehicle for the poem, an objectification of language, while the poet, solitary ego, puffs up in sacred power.

The single condition that unleashes the brute male power of poetry is that it be "directed." Poetry is masculine for Sartre insofar as it is concentrated, monolithic in sense and direction, insofar as it can be opposed to the occasionally fluid meandering of prose. All prose is directed to some degree, but it can appear as mere flaccid continuity; directed poetry, on the other hand, can only be the result of rare genius and unshakable determination. Sartre directly links the noncommitment of the poet to a form of femininity, to passivity ("The surrealist poet's irresponsibility follows immediately from his passivity. . . . The surrealists lie on their backs and float" [552]), but Genet's poetry, like Mallarmé's and Césaire's, finds itself totally, consciously engaged in its author's situation. Genet, like Césaire, makes surrealism work, makes it efficient. Despite Genet's original objectification, there exists in him a tremendous will to break through, to break out, which in the end gives his work an immense dynamic power. His poems finally ignite explosively, as did Mallarmé's; his writing serves as a means of transcending his situation and his constituted being.

The beauty of Genet's writing, as Sartre sees it, is not gratuitous, not thrown in as part of the bargain.[9] It is a

8. The image is reminiscent of the speech in *Les Mouches* in which Orestes speaks of Argos in terms of rape, as something "to be taken" (act 2, scene 1).

9. The changes in Sartre's concept of beauty could be traced back from *Saint Genet* to *Situations 1* and forward to *Plaidoyer pour les intellectuels,* where it is defined as the human condition presented as the product of the author's creative freedom.

tool and a morality, necessary in forcing the reader to re-
assume an imaginarily inverted world of evil. The source of
beauty is the unity of the work, which is based on Genet's
recreation of the self through art. Aesthetic intuition
appears to him as a road to salvation, and he follows it
with desperate obsession. The principles of his art are his
own fundamental desires, and the structures of his imaginary world are his needs and sensitivities. He pursues evil
with the persistent defiance of a sulky child, but "when a
systematized, hardened sulking holds out for ten years,
thirty years, when it is at the root of the most singular, the
most beautiful of poetic achievements, when it changes
into a world system, into an occult religion, then it must
singularly transcend the level of a simple childish reaction,
a man's freedom must be thoroughly involved in it" (63).
Conscious direction, intuitive authenticity, the refusal of
gratuitousness, obsessional concentration, total commitment and responsibility: these characteristics make poetry
far different from what Sartre conceived it to be at first,
and they redefine what Genet is. In Genet's hand, poetry
becomes a tool to change reality.

Genet represents a case of Sartrian heroism at the point
of impossibility. More radically and truly an exile from
language, society, and reality than either the black or the
peasant, Genet, in his solitude, is an extreme of human
existence. Genet is more alone than anyone, and in this
fact Sartre finds the universality of his works.

Genet's enterprise is based on the cementing of contradictions that cannot be resolved. Wanting to be at once
object and subject, the Other and himself, Genet combines
the two divergent forces in himself without synthesis. This
impossible unification exists only as an unattainable limit
point, the end of the movement that defines Genet. In

Genet there is no possibility of synthesis, and his history consists of an unfinishing, nonprogressing, circular movement
between thesis and antithesis, simultaneously affirmed.
His mind functions by what Sartre calls "tourniquets,"
whirligigs, rapidly twirling perversions of logic that embrace irreconcilable contradictions, spinning on an eternal
merry-go-round. For example, he can speak of himself as
"Jean Genet, the strongest of all and the weakest"—"the
strongest of all when he is the weakest, the weakest when
he is the strongest. He will enjoy the double pleasure of
sadism and masochism, not in the alternating or composite
form that psychoanalysts call sadomasochism, but simultaneously. His sadism is the secret dimension of his masochism and vice versa" (360).

The instrument of Genet's impossible unification, and of
his liberation, is, of course, language, "the false unity of
the Word" (360). Condemned by language, Genet liberates
himself through language and reinvents literature. He
achieves a "verbal" victory and his work becomes "an
ascetic experience which is achieved by the Word and
whose fulfillment is to dissolve language into silence"
(603). His future project can be thereby predicted as a
meditation of that "pure verbal symphony which is to give
an equivalent of silence and in which the only temporality
will be that of the 'vibratory disappearance' of the universe. . . . One can understand his not yet knowing
whether he is going to speak or remain silent: on this level
of abstraction speech and silence are one and the same. It
is Genet who can write the 'Mallarméan novel' of which
Blanchot once spoke" (621).

There is one common characteristic of the two forces in
Genet: they both function in the imaginary. As an adolescent, Genet allows his basic realism to give way to a state
of dreaming, of incommunicable fantasy and poetry; when

he realizes he has become a dreamer, he experiences a
liberating shock, and he decides to become the poet. He
first writes for his own pleasure, and then writing uncovers
for him readers and reciprocity. His writing develops from
an autistic, solitary onanism, from ceremonial gesturing, to
an attack on the world that has a real effect. He remakes
the world in an inverse sense for his readers; he finds its
justification, its origin and its sense in language, understood as beauty.

> What exactly happens? Is the real annihilated in signifi-
> cations? Does the contingency of being give way to
> necessity? Both. For language, as Blanchot has ob-
> served, is both the flight of being into significations
> and the evaporation of significations, in short, annihila-
> tion—and it is also *being,* whipped air, written, engraved
> words. Engaged, like the surrealists, in a process of
> demolition, Genet must, like them, construct a war
> machine in order to achieve his ends; and this machine
> has two faces, one of shadow and the other of light: it
> is the evil sacrifice of being to nothing, but it is also
> inclusion of nothingness in being. It attempts to dis-
> solve reality, but it salvages nonbeing. [599]

Genet awakens from a dream to lucid action, his gestures
give way to acts; by one decision, the decision to write, he
begins to liberate and to create himself, to change his
world and reinvent his reality. Literary creation, first a gesture, an imaginary act, becomes in him more and more a
real act: the totalization of the self. Language, born un-
spoken in the back of Genet's throat, used to create an
imaginary reality, necessarily reasserts itself as praxis.

  Genet first writes to affirm his solitude. In Sartre's view,
one is never alone as long as one's thoughts remain com-
municable, for all men are "in-society," so long as they act

as though judged by a secret tribunal formed in the world around them, so long as they reach for the good. True solitude, however, exists in all men as negativity; it is neither subjectivity nor objectivity but their interrelation experienced as failure. Solitude is born, in the midst of communication, in the incommunicable part of all thought. The criminal and the madman, then, are truly alone; they are

> pure objects and solitary subjects; their frantic subjectivity is carried to the point of solipsism at the moment when they are reduced for others to the state of a pure, manipulated thing, of a pure *being-there* without a future, prisoners who are dressed and undressed, who are spoon-fed. On the one hand are dream, autism, absence; on the other, the ant heap; on the one hand, shame and the impotent hatred that turns against itself and vainly defies the heavens, and on the other the opaque being of the pebble, the "human material." The man who becomes aware of this explosive contradiction within himself knows true solitude, that of the monster; botched by Nature and Society, he lives radically, to the point of impossibility, the latent, larval solitude which is ours and which we try to ignore. [636-37]

Genet is such a person. Chosen victim of society, Genet universalizes all men's solitude: "Our solitude carried to the point of Passion" (644).

4

L'Idiot de la Famille

> . . . le plus objectif des écrivains veut être une présence in-
> visible mais *sentie* dans ses livres. Il le veut et, d'ailleurs, ne
> peut faire qu'il ne soit tel.
>
> *Plaidoyer pour les intellectuels*

Through *Qu'est-ce que la littérature?* and *Baudelaire* Sartre
developed a moral setting for the writer, based on a
masculine-oriented theory of transcendence. The writer's
function was social action in the "arid desert of the objective world"; his task was, in part, to resist the erosive and
engulfing flow of the feminine, to dry out the moist presence of the maternal within him. *Saint Genet* represents, in
a way, the culmination of this movement in Sartre's criticism. Although many of Sartre's positions have broadened
or changed, still the drive to transcendence that Sartre
looks for is found most clearly in Genet, and *Saint Genet*
is the height of a would-be objective but highly personal
criticism that finds truest expression in the intensity of
negation.

So Sartre's latest work, an immense study of Gustave
Flaubert entitled *L'Idiot de la famille* (1971–72), seems a
departure from the militancy of all that came before.
Immediately striking are radical differences in style and in
Sartre's attitude towards Flaubert, his political enemy.
While *Saint Genet* is not always an attractive work, it is
still the best example of a certain art form, masked as

criticism; it spins wildly in contorted, intricate spirals, yet fits neatly (perhaps too neatly) into the Sartrian system. At first glimpse *L'Idiot de la famille,* published twenty years later, seems comparatively calm and passionless, the antithesis of a work of art. In the years immediately following the completion of *Saint Genet* Sartre became convinced that Marxism is "the philosophy of our time," and will not be surpassed as long as we live in a world of alienation and exploitation. When we have gone beyond scarcity a philosophy of liberty will be possible, but until then existentialism can only be a heuristic technique applied to Marxism, whose methods of analysis must be the basis of all present studies of man. In *Questions de méthode,* the essay that introduces Sartre's neo-Marxist *Critique de la raison dialectique,* Sartre proposed a structural and historical anthropology, which would serve as a tool in the development of Marxism by combining Freudian and existentialist insights with Marxist methodology. As *Baudelaire* and *Saint Genet* were conceived of as working examples of existential psychoanalysis, so *L'Idiot de la famille* undertakes an "anthropological" study of Flaubert, and its goal is to build towards a theory and a practice. As a result, in *L'Idiot,* immediate emotional appeal and content have been thinned out, "breaches of faith" and sleight-of-hand eliminated; the methodology is precise, clear, and consistent, following the outlines established in *Questions de méthode,* and argument and development are relatively simple and straightforward. To counter this potential accessibility, *L'Idiot,* like *Saint Genet,* is unfortunately—disastrously, in this case—long and repetitive; unlike *Saint Genet,* it is, for the most part, carelessly written and flat. Over the more than fifteen years that he has worked on *L'Idiot* without completing it, Sartre has lost his taste for it. In reasonable doses *L'Idiot* is a pleasure to read, and some parts are endlessly fascinating, but they are stranded in three thousand pages of swollen exposition.

Sartre set the grounds for elements of this style in two texts that date from 1965, in the heyday of the system-oriented theories of Parisian structuralism, when he had already been working on *L'Idiot* for a number of years. In three lectures in Tokyo, reprinted as *Plaidoyer pour les intellectuels,* Sartre seems to return after *Les Mots* to a view of the writer as a privileged being. Unlike others, the writer is an intellectual not by accident but in his essence. The very nature of his calling confronts him directly with the contradictions of human reality, and like all intellectuals he is alone, without a mandate, inassimilable, excluded, like Jean-Paul in *Les Mots,* "voyageur sans billet." The modern writer, moreover, is now perceived in a very different light from that of 1948, as Sartre defines him as "a poet who declares himself prosateur" (87).[1] That is, the writer is a man who uses everyday language and who appears to have something to say, like everyone else. But common language, as opposed to technical, specialized languages, is not geared to delivering information. In fact, it contains a maximum of "disinformation"; it supplies an overabundance of meanings and resonances, each of its terms has too much of a history, there is too much self-reference and mutual reflection between terms for it to serve as a direct vehicle of a clear content. It is for this that the modern writer uses it: the foundation of modern literature is ambivalence. He seizes upon the materiality of language as it seems to possess an independent life that escapes the writer. His art is to call attention to language as language, to language as a system that speaks through the writer and betrays his intentions by saying something

1. *Plaidoyer pour les intellectuels* (Paris: Gallimard [Idées], 1972). My translations.

other than what he thought to say. He uses sentences as "agents of ambiguity," and his basic task is to work on the nonsignifying elements of discourse (its materiality) in search of a sense. In other words, he has something to say, but that something is nothing one can say, nothing conceptual or signifying. What he communicates is not objective knowledge, but its opposite: silence, *nothing,* all of human existence through the totalization of a particular existence. He has nothing to say; he manifests everything.

The writer proposes silence with words. He does so by means of style, by trying to communicate the incommunicable. The literary work of art cannot be a direct cognitive message, it is not "life addressing itself directly to life and seeking to realize through emotion, carnal desire, etc., a symbiosis of author and reader" (105), but it does invite the reader to freely assume his own life "not by moralizing but, on the contrary, insofar as it requires of him an aesthetic effort" (105). Style does not communicate knowledge; it is, instead, all of language taking the point of view of a singular existence, a presentation of being-in-the-world that reveals the singular and the universal, the situation of the author in the social world and his entire epoch.

In a 1965 interview on the subject of "L'Ecrivain et sa langue,"[2] Sartre indicated that the various forms of language can be understood as though laid out on a scale

2. Reprinted in *Situations 9*, pp. 40–83. Translated by J. A. Underwood and John Calder in a collection of Sartre's essays called *Politics and Literature* (London: Calder and Boyars, 1973). Page references to that translation (with small changes) follow in the text. A third text should be added here: an interview with Michel Contat in the *New York Review* 22, no. 13 (Aug. 7, 1975): 10–17, which was published after the completion of this book and which confirms and restates much of what we have seen. Most particularly, it returns to the idea of true fictions and fictional truths, links objective truth directly to subjective thought and "le vécu" and meaning to total context rather than explicit signification, and offers an understanding of style as going beyond simplicity to become "the literary manner of presenting an idea or a reality" and "plurality of meaning." It also speaks of *L'Idiot* as the product of a personal style.

running from language as praxis and reciprocity to language as magic and masturbation. At one end there is scientific language, which is "pure practical" action and excludes any reference to man, and philosophical language, which is pure communication, seeking the reality of lived experience (*le vécu*). At the other end of the scale there is poetry, which Sartre considers a narcissistically arrested moment in the development of language. For him, poetry is verbal infancy, it means building sand castles with words for the beauty of it and not with the aim of communicating: it is language understood as magic, creation-appropriation. Poetry is retrospective (*fondative*), marking death in life, it is contraction and retraction, while prose is "prospective," tied to the future, acting in reality as expansion and dilatation. Prose, Sartre declares, is the *dépassement* of poetry. "Prose is continually having to rediscover and reestablish itself as against poetry: poetry is that which is transcended or dominated in prose" (100).

Although Sartre's revised definitions of poetry and prose are still highly debatable, they contain interesting implications. The terms of his argument are developed from *Qu'est-ce que la littérature?* and there the presence of poetry within prose was considered "néfaste." But now Sartre accepts poetry as necessary within prose: "In every writer there is still the child whose aim is not communication but precisely this kind of creation-appropriation" (80). Although theoretically the author can be considered as either *écrivain* ("writer") or *écrivant* ("one who writes"), poet or communicator, the true writer, Sartre says, is "l'écrivain écrivant," the "writer who writes," in whom both elements are present at once. Man first reacts to language in a proprietary fashion, using it as an external reality, through which he childishly attempts to appropriate the world; it is the given, in which he is immersed and which threatens to drown him. The poet remains fixed at this point, and language structures his world. But the true writer, according to Sartre, surpasses this stage to understand language as a collective means of communication. For "l'écrivain écrivant" the goal of literature is communication, but there always remains in his writing the residue of childhood, which causes words to light each other up, suggesting the absent, hinting at a sense beyond the signified. In the act of communication the incommunicable, the mysterious, is evoked through suggestion, multiple determination, and resonance. There is no thought beyond the bounds of expression. "Everything is expressible provided you find the right expression for it" (88).

Intimacy and mystery, the infantile and the maternal, then, have their valid place in prose. Such is the new understanding Sartre offers of his own critical style: he writes, he says, a "literary prose," which we are to perceive as lying halfway between the languages of philosophy and poetry. His "prose littéraire" begins as an effort at the pure communication of philosophy, at the communication of thoughts by signs, but it is nonetheless communication formed *in a particular way,* a semiappropriation of the world he creates through a personal style. In other words, in all his prose other than the pure technical exercise of philosophy, in all his writing that intends eventually to concern itself with that which is human, Sartre now admits the legitimate function of style. Prose literature, he now sees, cannot be understood only as what it signifies, for true communion between men must deal with men in their wholeness, through the mediation of language as a whole, without excluding the idiosyncratic, the personal, or the infantile elements of either.

Within this framework, *L'Idiot de la famille* might be viewed as a rounder, fuller approach to criticism. Sartre seems to have passed beyond the imperialistic and intensely aggressive criticism that occupied him for so long, and no longer must his argument be so consciously and deliberately weighted. In his early essays, he conceived of criticism as a hazardous enterprise, a risk shared with the writer, that demanded heroic courage and explicit commitment, but criticism in *L'Idiot* consists of the careful elaboration of a method, documentation and deliberation, combined with imagination. *L'Idiot de la famille* is emotionally slacker and less pointed than previous works; Sartre's message comes through without having to be so painfully etched in acid. Because *L'Idiot* is written "in a particular way," its sense is carried implicitly in each resonance, its meaning is embodied in its form. Sartre no longer needs to use language as a form of rape.[3] Thus, *L'Idiot de la famille* can be seen as a first acceptance of the self, a gradual, graceful yielding to the immanent, a partial return to equilibrium.

Unfortunately, this view affords only a very limited understanding of *L'Idiot*. The impulses of 1940 are still very much alive in Sartre in 1972. In an interview in *Le Monde,* published simultaneously with the first two volumes of *L'Idiot de la famille,* he said of the form of his work, "The style of the *Flaubert* is exactly what I wanted since I did not want to take any trouble. One ought to write books like this one without ever letting a concern with style predominate. Style belongs to Flaubert; it would be madness to write with style about a writer who spent his life looking for nothing else than style. Why lose time composing beautiful sentences?"[4] As in "L'homme ligoté," the idea here is that one must prefer thoughts to

3. See Ehrmann, "Of Rats and Men," where "Sartrian rhetoric" is presented as a series of ruptures and surgings, an uncertain combat in which reason becomes invective and passion becomes logic, a willed disequilibrium in which language becomes the rape of the reader. See also Fredric Jameson's *Sartre, The Origins of a Style* (New Haven: Yale University Press, 1961).

4. *Le Monde,* May 14, 1971, p. 20.

words, ideas to style, and that beauty is thrown in as part of the bargain.

In reducing style to the search for "belles phrases," Sartre makes clear his ambivalent attitude. While, theoretically, he has admitted the necessary presence of poetry within prose, the inevitability of style, and the unconscious infiltration of beauty into the hard grain of his writing, while, theoretically he has opened himself once again to the feminine and infantile elements of creativity, still he insists, on an immediate level, on an impulsively masculine, aggressive rejection of style and a partial contempt for the stylist. Flaubert has style, and, in fact, wasted his life looking for it, but Sartre has no time to lose on such trivia. Beautiful phrases may occasionally slip into the text, but he has no intention of using them to trick the reader. Beauty should be imperceptible, ephemeral, inessential to the argument. From this viewpoint Sartre's attitude has changed very little over twenty-five years: let the women fuss over style, if they must; the function of the male writer, totalizer, is still "to call a spade a spade."

The same ambivalence appears in Sartre's attitude towards Flaubert. For years Sartre attacked Flaubert as the very type of the despicably uncommitted bourgeois writer, who wrote to rid himself of both men and things; Flaubert's realism tranquilized, immobilized, and sterilized reality, it was death stalking the living by categories. Wherever he went, the grass no longer grew. Sartre saw Flaubert's writing as epitomizing the rentier's perversion of art for art's sake and held him responsible for the repression that followed the Paris Commune, because he did not write one word against it and because he consistently and ignobly attacked the working class. In *Questions de méthode* he began to change his attitude and wrote of Flaubert's "literary commitment," but as late as 1964 he explained his interest in Flaubert by the fact that Flaubert is his very opposite. Flaubert is also Genet's opposite: he is the man who dares not live things through to the end.

In the preface to *L'Idiot de la famille,* however, Sartre claims that, since 1943, "my original antipathy has changed into *empathy,* the only requisite attitude for comprehension" (8). No longer, Sartre feels, does he approach Flaubert with personal distaste, nor with a predetermined moral and political opposition, no longer does he have a "score to settle," for he has overcome his emotional involvement and polemic viewpoint for the sake of methodological precision. In fact, *L'Idiot de la famille* is written with more discretion and more apparent balance than previous works, and though it relies on fabulous reconstructions, still it is much more a calm exercise in the working out of a method, much more a proof by intelligent and well-documented argument than by persuasive misdirection. It is also proof by lengthiness: three thousand pages are simply too much to argue with. As Sartre explains in *Questions de méthode,* existentialism is to be applied here as a technique which will concern itself with mediations between historical forces and individual choice, with the point of insertion of the individual in his class. It is not enough to know Flaubert's birthdate and social status. We must know about Flaubert that, unlike his contemporary, Baudelaire, he is fixed on his father, a bitingly ironic, moody man, an atheist, a surgeon who rose through the ranks of the bourgeoisie directly from a peasant village, and who rejected his son as an incompetent at an early age when he showed himself slow in learning to read. We must know that Flaubert's mother came from a different social class, that she was religious, that she wanted her second son to be a girl, that Flaubert had an older brother and a younger sister, that his sister learned to read before he did, that they played together near the rooms used for dissection. Beyond that, we must understand how these relationships fit into group structures, how Flaubert appears within his class and how he perceived his class, how he understood his society, how he saw himself within his family, what his childhood was like and how he felt about it, how each member of the family related to him, how the family lived the ideologies of its class and epoch, what groups Flaubert belonged to in one way or another, what books he read, how he read, what reading meant in the 1830s, what it meant to be a surgeon's second son, a rentier, and so on. In other words, we must pinpoint through a continual cross-reference how Flaubert lived his situation, how the concrete touches the general. In a method that is analytic and regressive, as it studies Flaubert in his epoch, and synthetic and progressive, as it studies his project, we can hope to discover why Flaubert chose to write and why a certain public chose to make of him what it did. All this, Sartre would say, is the object of *L'Idiot;* its three thousand crowded pages do not intend to deliver a personal message, but constitute the necessary movement of an unfolding process.

But at the same time, in the *Le Monde* interview Sartre admits that although in *L'Idiot de la famille* he intends to suspend moral judgment on Flaubert (perhaps, he says, because he now understands how Flaubert suffered), although he accepts Flaubert as a man and not as a caricatural enemy, still there is throughout the book a constant attack on the bourgeoisie of the period and on the Flauberts as their representatives, still he dislikes Flaubert's characters; and he continues to approach the subject with certain ingrained attitudes, which he cannot always transcend. "It occurs that, on reading my texts, I find things I've written that strike me as having slipped out, I mean elements where I betray myself in spite of myself. Thus empathy is always possible, but it has its limits."[5]

5. Ibid., p. 21.

To understand *L'Idiot de la famille* it is necessary to measure the impact and visibility of its double nature. The critical approach is dictated by Sartre: to grasp the work as a whole, one must see it as both a negation and a restatement of the Sartrian *oeuvre*. Specifically, we must bring into focus the function of a new critical form (which implies both a tightening of method and a broadening of approach) and, withal, the continued presence of basic Sartrian schemata.

For example, constant throughout Sartre's criticism is the regulating principle of resistance against the flow of erosion, the struggle for definition, expressed in the theme of the transcendent male erection from the feminine mud of nature, from the formless, the damp, the intimate, from immanence.[6] We have seen Sartre use this schema in passages already cited. In reference to Baudelaire: "When he felt nature—the nature which belonged to everybody—rising and taking possession of him like a flood, he went rigid and taut holding his head above water [*il se crispe et se raidit, il tient la tête hors de l'eau*]. . . . Baudelaire chose not to be nature, to be the perpetual jarring refusal [*ce refus perpétuel et crispé*] of his 'natural self,' the head that stuck out of the water, watching it rise with a mixture of terror and disdain" (*Baudelaire,* p. 106). But this haughty stiffness is only self-deception, because Baudelaire's dandy is a myth. Sartre attacks Baudelaire because this defense fails, because in the end Baudelaire has yielded to the erosion of the immanent, accepted the given, and has never purified himself of the maternal element within him. His life has sunk into the vegetable dimness of the past; it is a very slow and painful decomposition.

In *Saint Genet,* the moral imperative of transcendence becomes sexually diverted, confused, but the thematic

6. See R. G. Cohn, "Sartre's First Novel: *La Nausée*," *Yale French Studies* 1, no. 1 (1948): 62–65, for a view of this theme in *La Nausée*.

obsession remains the same. In wrestling with evil, crime, and homosexuality, in trying to think them abstractly, and in comprehending the particular mode of Genet's obdurate resistance, Sartre must, of necessity, change the terms of his analysis. But the message remains clear: keep your head up, stand firm and dry and erect. "Genet remains standing, stiff, bristling, determined to keep his head above water." (Genet debout, raide, hérissé s'applique à tenir la tête hors de l'eau.) Genet holds on, an immovable rock, in the torrent of socialized language that flows past him; he never lets himself go.

In *L'Idiot de la famille* Sartre first uses this pattern of images to characterize Flaubert's resistance to his bourgeois destiny, "the implacable slipping which sweeps him away" (1658), and to the flow of time. "He clings desperately to his adolescence . . . anything rather than arrive at manhood. He clenches [*il se crispe*]; compressed, knotted, his muscles wear themselves out fighting against time" (1658).[7] But, as was the case with the "sulking child" Baudelaire, all that is achieved is a sand castle, menaced by a rising tide. After the crisis of Pont-L'Evêque, Flaubert gives way: "After 1844, [time] is a slow river carrying him *towards destruction*. That is, the immutable, by dint of being tossed about by the currents, passively undergoes the slow deformations imposed on it from the outside: inert, exterior forces destroy it without its being able to resist them" (1882).

But more than that, Sartre makes use of this pattern again to explain a major unifying scheme of Flaubert's life and imagination, the theme of "negative verticality." First visible in Flaubert's adolescent writings (as the constant temptation of suicide by falling, jumping out a window, or

7. Page references following in the text refer in this first section of chapter 4 to volumes 1 and 2; the translations are my own.

off a cliff into the dark waters below, etc.), found again in his retelling of the legend of Saint Julian (where "the author, out of love, chooses for him the ultimate feminine form of death: drowning" [1857]), the theme finds extraordinary expression in the crisis of 1844, in Flaubert's fall and false death. In 1844 at Pont-L'Evêque, Flaubert succumbs to a fit, he falls and becomes an inert mass, a mineralized thing to be carried away, absolute passivity. Thus, this "dream of resignation, a desire to fall, to be reunited with the earth or water, with the original passivity of matter, minerality" (1857), constitutes the radical meaning of the crisis that was to be the central moment of his life. "At question was certainly a *resignation* represented by a loss of equilibrium and a falling into passivity. Falling has always signified for Flaubert, even in the crudest sense, the refusal of the human, a role too difficult to maintain, insofar as the status of humanity seems to him to coincide with the standing position, a symbol of activity" (1857). Here, one can no longer accuse Sartre of imperialistic criticism in terms of his imagery; for once, the language and imagery of the criticism seem to grow organically from the material, and their applicability is plausible. Concomitantly, the moral judgment no longer appears immediate and irrevocable; Sartre does indeed seem more concerned with comprehending Flaubert than with condemning him.

But the condemnation is nonetheless present, and it finds expression precisely through the permanence of certain vocabulary and schemata, certain recognizable linkages that continue to function in Sartre's writing. Sartre understands falling as a temptation for Flaubert, and he portrays the act of falling as a guilty, unmanly form of onanism, a weakness to be compared with the flight into the "effeminate" philosophy of immanence, the retreat into intimacy, which took place behind closed doors, in warmth and comfort. "Yes, I am sure that Flaubert allowed himself constantly to fall: in Paris, he would fall flat down on his bed, his eyes open, his boots on his feet; perhaps he gave himself the pleasure of falling on the floor. . . . These were solitary pleasures: he offered them to himself with the doors closed and for just a short while" (1857). Through the strange and delicious odor of decadence, the heated atmosphere of complicity, that he attaches to what must be understood as a relatively innocuous act, Sartre conveys a distinct attitude of dour moral disapproval. Flaubert's shameful solitary pleasures constitute an offense to Sartre's austerity, a lapse in human dignity, which Sartre will not condone. Empathy is possible, but it has its limits.

But Sartre's disapproval of Flaubert's general conduct is not the major focus of *L'Idiot de la famille*. The central problem of *L'Idiot* is that of imagination; the principal theme of the book is Flaubert's passivity. Behind the method of empathy, the careful documentation, the surface suspension of moral judgment, the loose strands of *L'Idiot* come together—through elements peripheral to its main function of analysis, separate from its stated theoretical intention—in a condemnation of Flaubert that is specifically focused on the inactive nature of his literary project. In *Qu'est-ce que la littérature?* passivity was considered the antithesis of creative liberty and commitment, and Sartre has always considered it incompatible with literature as an act of heroic virility. Despite *Les Mots,* where Sartre finally denied that writing was heroism, this theory has significant continuation in *L'Idiot* and constitutes its organizing paradox: "Art is an act, Gustave is only passion" (2105). What *L'Idiot de la famille* asks can be formulated along these lines: how does Flaubert, man of failure (*homme-échec*), relative being, "passive agent," deal with the discovery that art is an act?

The question of passivity has always been crucial for Sartre. Its first meaning for him begins in Husserl's concept of passive synthesis and passive genesis.[8] For Husserl, the physical thing is given in passive intuition to consciousness, and synthesized there in a unitary flow prior to any active synthesis. This passive constitutive genesis is prelogical and prepractical; it presents, on the lowest level, an environment of "objects" to the ego, upon which all action must be based. In an early essay, Sartre explained that Husserl distinguishes between "passive syntheses arising from association and whose form is the flow of time and active syntheses (judgment, fiction, etc.)."[9] In Sartre's eyes, every fiction was, then, an active synthesis, a product of our free spontaneity, and every perception a purely passive synthesis.[10]

Husserl's theory is at the root of *L'Idiot,* and especially at the root of its metaphysics, in the opposition of pathos and praxis, of passion and action. The metaphysics of passion, for Sartre, bases itself on the acceptance or sufferance

8. See Husserl, *Cartesian Meditations,* trans. Dorian Cairns (The Hague: Martinus Nijhoff, 1960), pp. 77–81.

9. *L'Imagination* (Paris: Presses Universitaires de France, reprint ed., 1969), p. 157. Sartre envisages *L'Idiot* in part as correction of his early work on the imaginary mode of consciousness. The theme is clearly crucial to Sartre's thought, and many philosophers and critics are now returning to his early works with interest. Both there and in *L'Idiot,* Husserl's theories are of central importance; constitution, passive synthesis, empathy, egology, and other important concepts in *L'Idiot* are taken from Husserl.

10. There are obvious resonances of this theory throughout Sartre's thought. It has clear influence on his understanding of immanence and transcendence as being and doing, on his conception of interiority as a moistly passive flow, and on his view of poetry as a retreat into the self, into the past. It clarifies, too, the important opposition of the verbs *agir* and *pâtir* ("to act" and "to suffer") and the adjective *pâteux* ("pasty") in Sartre's fiction, as well as the image of the viscous paste (*pâte*) into which all masculine precision threatens to sink (for example, the malicious, premasticated, homosexual paste-universe of Proust and Daniel Sereno).

of the nocturnal, oneiric world of failure (as poetry is based
on the failure of language); in *L'Idiot,* Sartre describes
Christ's Passion as a "sacred passivity" (1385), which reveals to us our exile and our "being-towards-death" (Heidegger). Passion is a perversion of the liberating act of
negation, a perversion of the "solar world where life
appears as the supreme good and death as the supreme
evil" (1388). As it tends to the imaginary, it becomes false,
illusory, dark, and incomplete. As the romantics used it, it
is the world turned inside out, where death, madness, and
passion take the place of their opposites.

In *L'Idiot,* as in Sartre's previous works, preanalytic
thought is described as bestial, emotional fluid, autistic,
and onanistic. It represents the functioning of a passivity
that ingests the given and the primacy of the feminine principle: "The *Animus* thinks, the *Anima* palpitates" (1067).
Praxis is an active, masculine synthesis, for the most
part; it is a lived surpassing of the feminine and the preanalytic, an aggressive taking hold of the world; it is the
complex and reciprocal relationship of men to the world
and to each other through their work on the world. *L'Idiot
de la famille* is itself conceived of in terms of this metaphysics; it combines what Sartre sees as masculine analysis
and projection with a passive, feminine submission to facts,
an acceptance of the given. Finally, the influences on
Flaubert are understood in this way: he inherits both a
masculine doubt and a feminine faith. From his surgeon
father alone he receives both an impulse toward a masculine "surgeon's eye," toward analysis, and an opposite
impulse toward the passive observation of realism and em-
pirical scientism, toward "a particular kind of waiting that
I shall term *feminine*" (445).

As for Flaubert himself, there is no question. "Gustave is
a woman" (446). He is made passive; his "vertigo," his

distaste for living and for all sorts of undertakings, his difficulty in denying or affirming anything, are signs of a
"passive constitution." From his first youth, he is characterized by passivity and lethargy (51), by the incapacity to
act, by a lack of (transcendent) ideas, and by a flight from
reality. The organizing theme of his life is the search for
absolute passivity, the attempt to reach the state of inert
materiality. Gustave, as a child, is not made for action. He
cannot act practically, yet he cannot become an inanimate
object. His domain is pathos, emotion experienced as pure
violence to which he is subjected but which he cannot
affirm himself.

Despite the multiple influences that shape Flaubert, the
social and familial milieu that constitutes his "predestina-
tion," it is specifically his mother who makes him passive.
As an infant, Flaubert is fashioned by the ever-present care
of his mother so as to interiorize maternal activity as his
own passivity; his mother embodies the "pathetic structure" of his affectivity. It is always the mother, Sartre says,
who determines the degree of pathos in the child: she
orients the child toward his angers and fears, to "the pre-
dominance of the *pathetic* (interior emotion which one
suffers) or of the *practical* (exteriorized violence and
tumultuous emotions which go beyond themselves to an
act of aggression)" (58-59).

In most children, frustrated needs lead them from internal, pathetic violences to aggression as a first form of
transcendence and social development. In Flaubert,
according to Sartre (in what he admits is an unprovable
"fable"), normal aggressivity was never given a chance to
develop. Caroline Flaubert must have been, in terms of this
hypothesis, a totally conscientious mother who never let
her son feel a single physical want or unsatisfied need; she
continually spoiled him, continually manipulated him. But,

at the same time, she never loved him. She never let him feel himself to be the end purpose of any attention or affection; he remained always nothing more than an object to be handled like a delicate instrument. Massaged, kneaded, he has neither rights nor love, neither torment nor value, and he absorbs action as a force to which one submits. He never develops either aggressiveness or a transcendent relationship with his mother based on reciprocal eroticism.

As a result, Flaubert remains locked in infancy for the rest of his life; like Baudelaire, "Gustave never went beyond his childhood" (56). He refuses to leave the protected world of the family circle for the threatening solitude of adulthood; unlike Genet, he works no change on reality. He refuses to compress his spirit into the narrow confines of responsibility; instead, in his adolescence, he indulges in repeated swoonings, that he understands as dissolution into nature and subhumanity. He takes refuge in the calm horizontality of the ocean; he liquefies himself to reduce resistance and to flow back to the mother. Sexually, he remains arrested at the stage of pathos just described: his basic desire is to be a helpless infant flat on his back, like the cadavers on his father's dissecting table, manipulated by the severe and somewhat masculine hands of his mother. If possible, he would change his sex, and make of himself a little girl that his mother would love.

Sartre discerns a definite social significance in Flaubert's passivity: it means an acquiescence to an already existent family hierarchy and social order. Although, as the son of a successful bourgeois surgeon, Flaubert looks down on most of society, within the family he understands himself as a lesser being ("moindre être"), a dependent vassal of his father, feudal lord, ranked below his older brother, who will inherit and continue the father's work. He chooses to accept this secondary status which has been imposed upon him. "Vassal and woman by his dependence and passivity, he prefers obeying to giving orders. Deciding, acting, giving, in sum, ruling, these are the affairs of the Lord" (725).

Flaubert's passivity, his dependent status and "moindre être," mean, of course, a choice of the feminine condition. He is a receptacle (as Genet was a receptacle, a spittoon), inessential, useless, gratuitous, a flat, placid pool; he is feminine submission, "vegetative" existence, patience, circularity and syncretism; like Jean-Paul, his role is theatrical, he must please and seduce; his being is in the hands of others. "What does he desire, if not to be the object of aggression, to become prey, to swoon beneath brutal caresses . . . to be moistened, impregnated, penetrated? And in the couples that he forms successively with the wind, the river, the sun, he is always designated by feminine substantives, and his partners are always masculine. . . . He is the earth . . . knowing quite well that the earth is a woman and woman is the earth in peasant religions" (685). His imagination is feminine; he sees himself as "the passive center of a fabulous and submissive universe made only for him" (921), as Genet was at the center of a "beau cosmos tout fait," and he substitutes for his "being-in-the-world" a "being-within-the-world," which is proper only to things.

His choice of femininity is a choice of continued domestic dependence and eternal adolescence, "the permanence of youth dreamed by passivity" (1675). In the crisis of Pont-L'Evêque, he realizes permanently the irresponsible condition of the adolescent supported by his family: "This chronic invalid is maintained by his illness in a state of extreme dependence, an accident has reduced him to the condition of a minor for eternity, in other words, to the feminine condition" (1867).

Sartre goes so far as to consider Flaubert's feminization

as irreversible, as castrating (in the psychoanalytic vocabulary he permits himself) because Flaubert will never be
capable, in any domain, of an act of "manly" aggressivity.
This figurative castration is repeated with different agents
in the early fall from his father's grace and in the family's
refusal of his first choice of a theatrical vocation. Its repetition puts into motion the process of Flaubert's self-
irrealization and his conversion to writing. To understand
that conversion, we must look at the second theme of
L'Idiot, with which Sartre introduces and constantly inter-
weaves the theme of passivity: the theme of language.

Passivity, according to Sartre, is a "private" state. It implies an imprisonment within the self, a flight from the
world; it is pure receptivity prior to any desire or means of
communication, "suffering without expression" (139).
The "active" emotion Sartre understands as "public"; it
begins in communication and reciprocity. In the communication of a need, in the expression of an idea, the child
reaches out and controls his environment through language.
Through aggressivity or love, he emerges into a linguistic
universe, which is the universe of the family and social
existence, to establish his sovereignty as man among men
by the practical mastery and use of words.

Because of his passive constitution, Flaubert has problems with language from the first. Sartre opens L'Idiot de
la famille with a discussion of Flaubert's slowness in learning to read. At the age of seven, he cannot comprehend,
from his father's explanations, the elementary relationships
between letters and between syllables that make words,
but at the age of nine he considers himself a playwright. In
that interval, he has chosen a career, and his choice is
based on his original painful relation to words.

Flaubert's difficulties with language, which make of him

the "idiot" of the family and cause his father to turn his back on him, originate in the deficiency of his relationship to the Other. He is, like Genet, an exile from language. His passive constitution means the absence of reciprocity, and this determines what language first is for him. "Language comes to him from the outside: the transcendent act of signifying is the operation of the Other and completes itself in a signification which determines it from without" (151). Instead of actively entering the linguistic universe, Flaubert receives language in predetermined blocks from others. Sartre says that Flaubert experienced a poor "insertion" into language: language is given to him, he regards it from the outside as a thing, as belonging to others. He focuses his attention on its material aspects, its sonority, and its sensuality, and ignores its intention, its meanings, and its uses.[11] He himself cannot be the originator of language, he has nothing to say, because he sees himself only as a valueless object, not capable of being the sovereign creator of meanings. He receives meanings, and self-meaning, from the Other. So, since all forms of speech are acts, and Flaubert refuses to initiate action, what we must understand is that "he *makes use* of words but he does not speak" (142):

> As long as no one thought of giving him a primer, nobody noticed that he does not speak but that he *is spoken*. But as soon as he has to learn to read, language transforms itself before his eyes: one has to decompose according to the rules, affirm, negate, communicate; what he has to be taught this time is not just the alphabet but also praxis, for which nothing has prepared

11. Sartre will consider this focus on materiality as a source of Flaubert's art: the multiple determination of meanings. The written word, Sartre says, remains always an inessential form of spoken language for Flaubert.

> him: the *pathetic* child approaches the sphere of the
> *practical* and discovers that he is not made for it. . . .
> He will read, he will write, but language will always
> remain for him that double, suspect being that talks
> to itself all alone inside him, filling him with incom-
> municable impressions, and that makes itself speak,
> demanding of Gustave that he communicate with
> others when, literally, he has nothing to communicate
> . . . the child finds himself to be *passive* in the *active*
> universe of discourse. [49–50]

Language represents the essential form of Flaubert's
alienation. As a child Flaubert can understand spoken
language only as the property of the *pater familias,* who
lends it out to each of his vassals. However, written language, where matter and form are radically distinct, where
the reader must actively create a meaning out of a group of
impersonal possibilities, cannot be understood as the
father's property: it implies universality and reciprocity.
To learn to read is to learn to act; in the beginning, Flaubert, who only knows how to obey, does not understand
what is being asked of him. Although he eventually learns
to read, he offers a passive resistance at first, because
reading means giving up his protected position within the
narrow circle, the deep well, that is his family. It means
"abandoning the anxious but tender inertia of lived experience [*l'inquiète mais douillette inertie du vécu*] to
become the cold and capable subject of an enterprise"
(364). He resists reading as he resists growing up.

"To the theme of language is opposed the theme of his
stupors" (32). In Flaubert's adolescent raptures, he becomes the oceans and the forests; he plays dead. Sartre
interprets these stupors (*hébétudes*) as defensive attempts
to return to the lost paradise that existed before he was
rejected by his father. Since his father's condemnation was

based on Flaubert's slowness in learning to read, the "hébétudes" are first of all an escape from language. They are also a flight from ideas, a denial of transcendence, and a retreat into the self. To flow into nature means metamorphosis into inert materiality and prelinguistic animality. The youthful Flaubert conceives of these semiidiotic states as poetic ecstasies, in which he experiences undifferentiated intuitions, which language is inadequate to express. He opposes poetry as felt emotion to language as analysis; language as analysis is to him decomposition and death, the betrayal of intuition. His first literary vocation is born of this theory:[12] he will be the inspired poet, the transcriber of dreams and of received cosmic ecstasy; his writing will be romantic abandon and masturbatory eloquence. Flaubert's passivity, which structures his world view, determines his original relationship to language and to literature. As part of a generalized *exis,* a flow of accepted habits, the literary experience for the young Flaubert is a noncreative expectation, a state of waiting (*attente*), a submission to and an ingestion of a text. He is hardly alone in his reading habits; Sartre claims that most of Flaubert's adolescent contemporaries dealt with romantic literature in this way. For his fellow schoolmates, the "collégiens," the experience of literature was based on a possession by the Other; the reader is filled to overflowing, enchanted, hypnotized by someone else's dream. "Bound, depoliticized, reduced to autism" (1379), the readers become impotence dreaming desire, and reading becomes a refusal of reality.

In its extreme form, passivity becomes autism. According

---

12. Later, in *Madame Bovary,* the influence of this theory is still apparent. Sartre cites the seduction scene in the woods, where Rodolphe is the means by which the cosmos enters Emma to create a privileged moment that is the death of language. Nature is mute; silence is authenticity. In *Saint Antoine,* Sartre interprets the final phrase, "être la matière!," as in part an attempt to return to an authentic prelinguistic universe.

to Sartre, passivity is the basic impulse in romantic literature, and the act of dreaming becomes powerful enough to
affect writer as well as reader. Because they do not reach
towards the real, because "they do not distinguish what is
from that which can be" (1378), basic desires become
imaginary and are given imaginary satisfaction; the author's
sincerity becomes imitation; creative liberty atrophies and
gives way to an illegitimate, iron necessity, a preestablished
order in which no detail may be changed. The romantic
poet, "scriptor," passively receives his poems; they are imprinted as inspiration on the wax of his soul.

For Sartre, romantic literature is essentially pathos. The
romantic idea is either ecstasy or anguish, or, in other
words, the incapacity to reason; the romantic hero, who
has chosen failure and Christ's Passion, represents always a
pathetic being-toward-death, and he sexually possesses the
reader. The romantic reader (and writer) in abandon lets
himself be dreamed, thought, existed, by another; this is
the first glorification of passivity, which founds romantic
oneirism and romantic poetry as pathetic types. The romantic hero himself suffers existence the way his creator
suffers his creation: he endures the rule of pathos, and his
experience is the "pâtir."

At a certain point, Flaubert comprehends the failure of
romanticism. He cannot live only within the moment of
poetic ecstasy, because, as a human being, he must communicate. "After the dream of a dream, born of a refusal
to communicate and a vain effort to recapture the solitude
of autism, there is a sickening return. . . . After the mo-
ments of ecstasy, one had to return to words" (1194-95).
In Sartre's estimation, this defeat is the basis of Flaubert's
art; the "secret" of his writing begins as eloquence "rejected by the Other" (885), a war between inspiration and
censorship, between improvisation and controlled "taste."

In his late adolescence, Flaubert turns away from romantic poetry and rejects inspiration, to make of himself a reflexive and critical artist, "artisan, carver, workman of art" (872). His poetry is a product of his constitution, which is necessarily modified as Flaubert matures. In over a thousand pages of text, Sartre shows how, from the first moment of stress, the initial personalizing contact with reality, Flaubert's art changes as he restructures his life. The defeat of the romantic poet coincides with the birth of the artist; the crisis of Pont-L'Evêque, the deciding moment in Flaubert's life, gives unity to his existence as, in part, a rejection of romanticism.

Writing itself changes Flaubert because it is unavoidably an act of personalization, lived against his family, against the given; it is a creative, contradictory, active struggle to invent his own way of living, perpetual totalization, a going beyond interiorized determination. Flaubert develops his illness, the "profound wound" of his constitution, he integrates it into lived experience through self-objectivization in a book. He cannot escape his constitution, but each moment is a retotalization of the self, lived at the level of stress. The mediating form of reunification for him is art, which he begins to live as an option, as "engagement."

We must remember that although the passive element predominates in Flaubert, Sartre has never seen him as pure passivity. Although Flaubert dreams of absolute passivity and irresponsibility, he cannot negate his humanity to become inert materiality. Despite his basic dependence, despite his bad faith, the attempted dissimulation of his own liberty, he is still free, and he must act and decide every day. According to Sartre, he functions, for the most part, on the level of the passive synthesis, that is, he avoids making obvious decisions, willed intellectual acts, and seeks to live on the basis of passively received, predetermined patterns of behavior; like the romantic hero, the unity of his subjective life is the "pâtir." Sartre defines him as "passive activity": he acts, but pretends to be only acted upon by his destiny; he makes daily decisions that he hides from himself, or understands only as the will of the Other. So, although he does not see himself as acting, he necessarily acts upon his constituted being as he lives it, personalizes it, and, eventually, assumes it. Sartre's implicit judgment, felt by anyone who reads *L'Idiot*, is that Flaubert *could* have transcended his feminine condition and, moreover, *should* have.

The first indications of the conversion, of personalization, lie in a change of attitude towards the unreal. Where once Flaubert turned to the imaginary only as the choice of an "idiot," a last resort, as did Genet, now he begins to value the unreal above all. At school, he plays a Rabelaisian comic character he names "le Garçon," and, for the first time, his *persona* becomes superhuman. Secondly, since the physical irrealization of his own body on the stage has been forbidden him by his father, he turns to literature, and words become the mediators between him and the unreal world; he begins to "write his dreams." "Projecting his imaginary self into the grapheme and, at that moment, making it imaginary while conserving its sumptuous materiality. . . . He incorporates himself in the materiality of the grapheme, and, for lack of reality, he will lend himself material weight by making himself into an 'other-object' in his own eyes" (928, 949). Writing for him is a first form of personalization, in the paroxysmic form of onanism: "To write, for him, is to unwind. . . . he creates himself in writing" (954, 957). He creates fictional characters whose function is to materialize and individualize the inarticulable, the unspeakable in his fundamental desires.

The radical transformation implicit in his new grasp of

the self illuminates for Flaubert his central intentions. In his new status, he takes control of the world to put it into books, to reduce it to words, to possess it and to destroy it. Between the ages of 13 and 14, he converts to literature because he understands that it makes him, as the "imaginary Lord of language" (967), the imaginary equal of God, because through it, he can create his own being. When he writes, he thinks he changes everything; he totalizes the universe through the totalization of the self, by confusing both of them in the objectified form of the text. He takes words for things (as do all writers, according to Sartre), and the word becomes world; language gives "to the real dispersion of the universe the imaginary unity of a *creation*" (961). "At once, the conversion is accomplished; it is a new moment of his *personalization,* he has found his *being:* since his Ego is none other than the totalized world, he will be the one who, in one movement, captures the infinite in words and constitutes his own person" (964).

Flaubert is now committed to a form of writing quite separate from his early romanticism. After his famous "crisis of taste"—the rejection, in his early career, of his first, flamboyant *Antoine* by his friends Bouilhet and Du Camp—he concerns himself with literature as a critical art, and the literary object becomes himself as *other*. The romantic poet based his product on failure, on the primacy of the subjective, but Flaubert as the artist institutes, he determines his own being objectively. Imagination is no longer to be thought of as an escape into the imaginary; it becomes for the artist an exact technique, justified by the work created, which aims at a certain practical end: the annihilation of the world, the devalorization of the real, through the totalization of the imaginary and the universalization of the case of Flaubert. "The imaginary is no longer mythical transposition, it becomes systematic lying"

(1510). Art develops from personal disasters; it seeks to totalize creation in order to show its emptiness and vanity. Flaubert constructs a sacred and imaginary universe that reflects his own self, that he understands as reality considered from the point of view of the unreal, the finite understood through the intuition of the absolute and the infinite.

The format of irrealization of self is now radically different, and it uses different (though still "feminine") methods, "tightening, condensation, summarizing of the universe" (973). For the artist that Flaubert has become, language is even more essential a problem than it was for the romantic poet, whose only task was to feel: the ecstatic experience of the totalized is no longer sufficient in itself; it must now be retotalized in words. Flaubert becomes "a content in search of a form" (975), a martyr to the impossibility of adequate expression. Literature is for him the highest form of suicide, especially realized in the leap into madness, the fall and false death of 1844.

Between 1835 and 1844, in the passage from adolescence to adulthood, Flaubert undergoes a number of personal influences, which direct him towards his final condition and "being." Bouilhet and Du Camp are there to curb his lyric extravagance in writing; his father to tell him he will not be a poet. He will, instead, be a lawyer, or a notary. There are his fellow collégiens, for whom he invents a new personality, not Byron but le Garçon-Pantagruel, whose defense is not poetic ecstasy but pitiless laughter. Finally, there is his other friend Le Poittevin, the aesthete, a living gratuitous work of art, whose masculine persona Flaubert incorporates to make himself semiandrogynous, to lend to his writing a measure of virility, mineralized durability like the dandy's. Through Le Poittevin, aesthetic superfluousness becomes an ideal, and impersonality, immobility, and gratuitousness becomes absolute imperatives.

Sartre develops at length the movement of Flaubert's personalization through these influences and the concomitant passage from poetry to art, from first person to third person, in the autobiographical cycle of writings of this period (*Mémoires d'un fou, Smarh, Novembre*). On these bases, through personalization as distantiation from the self, Flaubert establishes a firm and precise project, from which he will never stray: "He will be the Artist . . . workman on the imaginary" (1090). As we have observed, the essence of this project to objectify himself lies in a rejection of the romantic influence; art, as he now begins to understand it, requires an ethical effort (*travail*) that will lift the artist above passion. In other words, art is an act.

The discovery that art is an act is double-edged for Flaubert. On the one hand, it begins to justify for him his vocation in terms of his family's opinions, in terms of a morality that he disdains, but continues to apply: "In the Flaubert family, from father to son, one must work" (1596). In becoming an artist, Flaubert gives up what Sartre calls the "suspect quietism" of the poet to participate in the bourgeois work ethic, where art is a *pratique,* a daily struggle; it is his own work that Flaubert must objectify and crystallize in writing. On the other hand, given his passivity, the idea of art as a form of action seems to demand an enormous willed change in Flaubert. "In order to pass from the experience of poetry to the composed work, one must tear oneself away from rumination, find a style, decide, act. The discovery which terrified him, around 1840, was that the artist, in his own fashion, is a man of action" (1615). From the beginning of his conversion, Sartre says, Flaubert bridges the gap between his constitution and his vocation on the basis of his misunderstanding of language as *given.* "The rule of the game for Flaubert is that words are not invented: they are chosen from that great stable totality of established language, i.e., for him, the language of others" (1615). The task of the writer first seems impossible on this basis. The distance between ineffable intuition and quotidian, socialized language, the banal, collective tool of doctors and lawyers, the *lieu commun*, renders the artist's materials hostile and ill-adapted to his project. But Flaubert discovers a means of stealing language from its owners, a tool that makes art impossible: style. Through style, he can try to retotalize intuition, since style for him is the secret and imaginary goal of the written word, the silence within discourse, the silence of discourse, that which appears when one causes the "mute" part of language to speak, that which stirs up in each term by each of the others all its multiple, interpenetrating interpretations and uses them together. "In sum, it is the full usage of language, everything serves, everything signifies, and the direct meaning is no more than one of the functions of a supersignifying object. But, at the same time, it is its irrealization" (1616). It is not "le dire" that manifests thought or Flaubert's reveries, but "la manière de dire," not apparent content but total form. "Information lies within the domain of signs, but the *sense* of a work of the mind is communicated to us directly by its formal beauty" (1619).[13]

Style is the theft of language, the diversion of language from its practical ends that constitutes the process of making language imaginary, but it is only possible to understand it for Flaubert as beginning in submission. Flaubert accepts the given, and his essentially uninventive meditation on style does not mean to change language: it is only a spiritual exercise, a dream about words that suddenly becomes a confusion between words and dreams (2079). So, the *travail* implicit in the work of art is not foreign to

13. The similarities with Sartre's own recent theories of style are obvious, though Sartre does not accept the theory of the inadequacy of language.

Flaubert, because it is, in this light, essentially passive. Flaubert can still hide from himself his creative liberty, he can still deny the future. Art remains an *attente*. For the naturalist Buffon, genius was a "long patience"; for Flaubert, patience is the *sign* of genius, daily work the sign of faith and the grace of election.

After Flaubert's completion of secondary school work, his father forces him to choose a respectable career and to begin to study for it. Flaubert apparently resigns himself to becoming a lawyer; he obediently opens the Civil Code intending to read it, and, in that paradoxical moment, obedience becomes praxis, and his passive activity verges on becoming an enterprise. In order to study for a career, "one must tear oneself away from the tender [*douillette*] intimacy of vain refusal and live at the surface of the self, without complacency, in the arid desert of the objective world" (1699). To obey, he has to act, he has to actively synthesize the material on the page before him. This moment is a repetition of his reading lessons, and his reaction is the same: complete stupor. But here he cannot help making an eventual decision.

He is forced into action at a time when a negative act of revolt is still impossible for him but when he has begun to understand art as a conceivable form of action for him, as an *issue*. In 1841, he makes his first decision: to put off action, that is, to put off studying. But there is a deeper choice implied in this gesture. He has decided to fail. He has glimpsed the possibility of instituting his own being through radical failure. The only way out of bourgeois society, since he cannot rise above it, is to fall below it, to become irremediably *l'idiot de la famille*. He objectifies himself as a man of failure, "that is to say a hominid, an offspring of man created to accede to the human condition and who, by a monstrous anomaly, is kept in a state of

quasianimality" (1741). Through deculturation, he eradi-
cates himself as a full social being, he realizes emptiness
within himself: he takes a permanent vacation. A young
man dies; an old man is born.

Because Flaubert is incapable of revolution, he tries to
disappear. In 1844, at home from Paris on vacation, Flaubert realizes his fall somatically. The crisis is a form of
intentional conduct, an option he has been preparing for
four years. Since 1840, he has experienced what Sartre
calls the "preneurosis"—"headaches, nightmares, apathy
mixed with feverish agitation, anguish, resistance of his
whole being to time which flows and carries him with it"
(1669). The fundamental structure of the neurosis is auto-
suggestibility; his "hébétudes" are no longer a form of
escape, but a premonition of the crisis. His body has an
oracular function, which expresses his destiny, the voice of
the Other within him. To faint and fall into hysterical
paralysis, which is physically to express castration desires,
means also to become nothing, the irrealization of self.

Reality has become too pressing for Flaubert. If he
returns from Rouen to study in Paris, he does so in obedience to his father, but he also does so of his own will. He
cannot refuse to obey, because of his passivity; he cannot
obey, because that means the act of assuming a future that
disgusts him. He must find a way out. The crisis realizes his
option of failure: "It is no longer a question of suffering
passing, reparable failures, but of revealing to others and
to himself that he is a man of failure" (1812). What is
different about the crisis when it finally arrives is that
Flaubert understands it as irreversible. Unlike the repeated ceremonies of the preneurosis, the act of falling
into death and madness is a commitment to "the secret
and terrifying" necessity of maintaining this state.

In a regressive attempt to regain infant status, the helpless condition of the newborn, Flaubert only recreates his adolescence. But that is satisfactory, because it gives him the permanent status of passivity and femininity; he becomes an object that is cared for and loved. He can hide in the bosom of the feudal family; rentier, he is transformed into *domus,* man objectified as property. He achieves irrealization: "Gustave, flat on his back, inert in his brother's hands, realizes his old dream: to become altogether imaginary" (1846).

The distantiation from the self that frees Flaubert from his own reality becomes the positive end, the teleological intention, of the crisis: he breaks with the passionate eloquence of his first works to redefine himself as a writer; he breaks from immediate life *in order* to be reborn as an artist. Sartre understands Flaubert's neurosis as a "long patience," inseparable from the attente of art. "Writing becomes neurosis and neurosis literature" (1918). The crisis, then, is both a negative tactical response to the father, a parricide, and a positive strategic response, a commitment, to the problematic exigencies of art. Reaching for a radical metamorphosis, a new vision of art and beauty, he invents himself as artist.

The paralysis of Pont-L'Evêque represents a choice of subjectivity and noncommunication pushed to the extreme of autism, of passivity pushed to the point of death and the irrealization of self. At the same time, it is a choice of a literary art that claims to link men together by communicating significations and thoughts. This contradiction brings Sartre to the implicit question of his book: "The passive agent, submitting until death . . . to his own passivity, how can he become the *craftsman* of style, whom Flaubert describes in contemporaneous letters, and who forges his sentences on the anvil, with hammer blows, a striking symbol that Art is *work, action?*" (1972).

Flaubert, in 1844, is brought face to face with this problem. To deal with it, he has recourse to the paradox of language and silence that he developed in his adolescence. He divides language into aesthetic potential (the perception of the silence manifest in words), and practical signification; he focuses on its materiality to derealize its practical use and meaning. He forges a style on the systematic utilization of the nonsignifying elements of discourse (thus, we infer, inventing modern literature) with the intention of making language imaginary. After 1844, he has left himself only one activity, art, and one form of contact with reality, language. In destroying the reality of language, he destroys the world and his own reality.

He sees this radical ascesis as the one path to genius: "Dying to the world *is* to be reborn an artist" (1996). When everything is lost, one writes, and the style and imagination born of that moment are imprinted with its radical nature. Language, then, becomes an organized but gratuitous totality, and Flaubert, embodying the impossible condition of man, "profoundly conscious of the *uselessness* of the word, sets about dreaming it" (1997). In this way, Flaubert resolves the problem of action by avoiding it. "In this case, writing is not an act, it is a dream of the pen and the man of imagination does nothing but let words arrange themselves on the paper like the images of a dream. Style is thus not originally a quality to be acquired but the simple way in which the elements of discourse are ordered in the mind or under the pen when one loves them for themselves. Flaubert, in *L'Education,* is formal . . . the 'great' writer . . . is nothing else but a mediator. Everything is done through him but almost without his cooperation. The essential is that he should be an image himself" (1997).

Words organize themselves into dreams; they are given to the writer, and his only task is to transcribe them. His art limits itself to the confines of his passivity as a mediation between inspiration and realization, and style becomes language "such as it speaks all alone to the ears of an inspired listener who now has only to write under its dictation" (1999). Flaubert's desire to make himself the "craftsman" is ultimately misleading; in 1844, literature becomes not so much a labor, in the sense of changing the world, but a state of grace.

Flaubert cannot conceive of himself as creative or active, but he knows he must be an artist. To save himself, he resuscitates God and divine inspiration, but not as he first posited them: he renounces romantic inspiration. In Sartre's interpretation, romantic inspiration was positive— God inhabited the artist, whispered in his ear, poured through the artist to spill out on the page—but Flaubert's conception of inspiration is negative and founded on the absence of the divine. "Through a certain but unknown grace, which one must merit by patient humility, the moment comes when the absolute negative—that is, the perfect blank of the soul—*requires* that one set fire to all of language in order to place it before the world as its pure negation, through the realization of the unreal and the irrealization of the real . . . the Idea cannot demand its form before having irrealized the totality of language. God's role is that; the writer is only obedience" (2079).

What has happened to Flaubert is a true change, a re-entry into religion not foreseen in the preneurosis. In the dark night at Pont-L'Evêque, running to meet his doom, Flaubert was all at once brought to a halt: "Suddenly, gripped by the terror that the truth of this world is truly atrocious . . . he resuscitates his dead God and puts himself back into His hands. . . . Gustave calls the Father to his aid" (2083). The artist's being that he creates at this moment is thus a regression as well as a radical invention:

it is a return to religious ritual and to infantilism. Flaubert's artist works only to merit the gift of genius, inspiration from an absent God. His labor is essentially peine; he works to suffer, to deserve. "It is because he is *waiting*. He is waiting for the miracle which will let itself be caught by the trap of his despair and which will cause a flower to be born under his morose pen" (2094). The work of art is the product of *travail* and manna in the desert, miraculous chance in language and the gift of a feudal lord. The artist's work is a comedy that realizes the failure of language, the impossibility of the human condition in self-destruction and dehumanization; its function is to keep the artist in a state of *disponibilité* ("availability").

Here, according to Sartre, lies the heart of Flaubert's mauvaise foi. In avoiding the question of action, in fear of his own freedom, and unwilling to carry through his desires to the end, Flaubert manipulates himself to camouflage for himself his own creative pride, to distort the need for writing within him, so as to make the artist's point of view coincide with God's. He denatures art so far as to assimilate it to his condition of passive activity, so that the writer does nothing and wants nothing. To Sartre, despite all his comprehension of Flaubert's choice and reasons for choosing, art remains always praxis, or, at worst, a "mini-praxis": the only way Flaubert, as "passive agent," can be a writer is by misunderstanding literature.

The methodology of *L'Idiot* requires extension from the case of Flaubert to the society in which he lived. It is in the third volume of *L'Idiot* that the pendulum of Sartre's method swings to its farthest point away from Flaubert. The subject matter of the volume is Flaubert's "neurosis" (which Sartre has previously defined as an affirmation of "loser wins") studied in its social and historical context as the totalization of the characteristics of French literature in the second half of the nineteenth century and of society under the Second Empire. This means that Sartre wants to prove that with Flaubert, art becomes neurosis, that *l'art pour l'art* stood for an alienated form of art oriented toward failure, that society under Napoléon III was not only false but *imaginary,* and that Flaubert's neurotic vision expressed and foretold a "neurosis of the Objective Spirit" of his society. (Sartre defines the Objective Spirit as "Culture in its practico-inert form," that is, petrified thoughts and values enclosed in books that represent the totality of social imperatives imposed on the individual.)

The questions raised in the first part of volume 3 ("The objective neurosis") originate in a continued rejection of Flaubert's aesthetic principles. Before 1848, Sartre claims, Flaubert's "task" remains more a dream than an enterprise, and he writes from a neurotic compulsion directed toward the imaginary and the incommunicable. His early writings are incantatory and masturbatory; his motivations are subjective, idiosyncratic and pathological; and the norms of his aesthetics are only transpositions of his hysteria. How then, Sartre asks, could Flaubert have written *Madame Bovary,* which appears to us in no way a neurotic or morbid work? How could a neurotic have produced a work of such consistency, rationality, rigor, and density, so classically distant from the author himself? And how, since Flaubert remains faithful to his misanthropic aesthetic values, could his writing have been accepted by a general public (that is, "integrated into the Objective Spirit"), "in other words, how could the madness of an individual have become a collective madness, and better yet, the aesthetic justification of his epoch?" (32).

Sartre answers these last questions—leaving the first ones for *L'Idiot*'s final unpublished volume—in a way one might have expected. It is, of course, not Flaubert but his public that makes of him an objective critical mirror, an authentic witness of his time. Through a neurotic public Flaubert's subjective neurosis is objectified and universalized. The readers of 1850 can recognize themselves in Flaubert's work (even if they misunderstand him) because they view themselves and their history through a "false objectivity," because their society feeds on false ideas (of nature, human nature, etc.) and neurotic values. The Second Empire is an illusion, a façade for the developing power of the bourgeoisie. The emperor is an imitation Napoléon; his nobles and his marshals, even his army, are all false. The collective dream that is the empire corresponds to the false beauty of l'art pour l'art; they share a common source, and both are dependent on the reign of personal power. "Almost at once, Gustave created the literature of appearances, and Louis-Napoléon created the reign of pretence. The adaptation of one to the other is not fortuitous" (651).[14]

Flaubert's "deviation" acts as the measure of his society, as the tacit expression of the dominating and middle classes, and the aesthetic norms implicit in *Madame Bovary* are immediately grasped by, and imposed upon, the writers of his time. Through Flaubert, the contradictory imperatives of literature in the nineteenth century (inspiration-work, gratuitousness–practicality, etc.) come to be seen as impossible to resolve, and the artistic response to those contradictions can only be irrational and psychopathic. From 1850 to the beginning of the twentieth century, from the postromantic generation to the last symbolists, the operational imperative, the condition of writing, was neurosis (depersonalization, *impuissance*); to write, one

14. Volumes 1 and 2 of *L'Idiot* were published in 1971 and numbered pages 1–2136. Volume 3 was subsequently published in 1972 and numbered pages 1–665. All further page references in this chapter are to volume 3.

had to be mad, or at least one had to play at it. While the works produced in this period are not of a neurotic nature in themselves, the literary doctrines that produced them are, according to Sartre, and the act of reading in the Second Empire represents the sado-masochistic prolongation of neurotic experience.

The public rejected by the artist of 1850 can accept his work because to some degree that public rejects itself. "To be a bourgeois under the Empire, one must hate in oneself the bourgeois of the July Monarchy" (333). Sartre claims that the principle of art that Flaubert discovers is hatred of the self, which he shares with his public in the guise of hatred of the bourgeois and the worker. The bourgeois reader recognizes this hatred; he interiorizes it and redirects it as catharsis, as redemption from the failure of 1848. Hatred of the bourgeoisie and the self-hatred of the bourgeois artist imply a general misanthropy, since the bourgeois sees himself as the universal image of mankind. The artist's guilt leads directly to a larger desire to harm and to degrade, to deny man's transcendent nature: man can only be defined as an object to be exploited, to be devoured, as workable matter, "suffering passivity," inevitable failure. The intention of the artist in 1850, as Sartre sees it, is self-destructive, pessimistic, nihilistic, criminal, misanthropic, homicidal, and even genocidal. His literary act confirms the misanthropic ideology of scientism (which Sartre calls a "disguised dream of genocide"), defends the rights of property and capital, seeks to replace God by the "human Thing," and justifies exploitation and alienation. "A work of hatred—that is, one that takes hatred as its point of view—*speaks the truth of the epoch*" (323); the Second Empire is only an eighteen-year-long dream of evil and hate.

For Sartre, the liberal period of the Second Empire is,

more than any other, Flaubert's society, and the end of
the reign of Napoléon III on the fourth of September 1870
marks the beginning of a long agony, in which Flaubert
survives himself as a living fossil. Flaubert makes the
Second Empire his society because it elevates him to an
imaginary aristocracy. The victory of the Prussians plunges
him back into "muddy" bourgeois reality; it means for
him the violation of his rights as a proprietor, the end of
the Latin world, the triumph of science and the symbolic
father, but more than that it signifies the triumph of reality and the failure of failure, the disqualification of the
unreal. The defeat of the French army at Sedan is "the
refutation of his entire existence and the abolition of the
failure-catharsis he chose in 1844" (581), his "realization,"
his awakening to and coincidence with his facticity and
finitude. The imaginary was only a ruse of the real; the impossible flight from being is now reflected in the eyes of
others as mere weakness, and the real intrusion of the
other into the prison of his dreams returns Flaubert to a
world of praxis, where language can no longer be "de-
realized." The nonsignifying elements of language give way
to real signs, and the utilitarian values of the bourgeoisie
are reinstalled in Flaubert. He becomes once again the
family idiot, "un rêve de cloporte," denounced as unfit by
the efficient Prussian technocrats and the practitioners of
the Flaubert family, and he must now see his former art as
a crime, responsible in part for the radical inefficiency and
impotence of the empire. Flaubert's crisis of 1844—which
in some measure was an act of defiance—prophesied and
called for the Second Empire. It reopened a cycle closed at
Sedan: the fall of the Second Empire is the father's final
and long-awaited revenge.

Sartre's ideas in this third volume come across rather

unhappily in paraphrase. They make somewhat more sense if one places them within the Marxist-existentialist framework of his recent thought, where *any* society based on the division of labor and exploitation has an objective but false understanding of itself, a self-justifying ideology, where any elaborated ideology is an unavoidable falsification of nonverbal intuition, and where language is an immediate betrayal of praxis. Sartre does, moreover, make some effort here to seem objective. He tells us that there is no negative intention, no depreciation, in his definition of ideology as a mineralized, petrified, and passive form of thought, and if he has said that in 1850 literature defines itself as inhuman and feminine, as the choice of impotent men, feminized misogynists, if that literature negates praxis and affirms pathos and failure, still, "these remarks are not intended to condemn a priori the works that will be born of this postulation of inhumanity proper to the writers of the second half of the last century. On the contrary, some of them are among the most beautiful in our literature" (172).

Yet there is still something quite strange and unfriendly about what Sartre has to say, despite the image of grudging generosity and mild evenhandedness he offers us. Even before parts of *L'Idiot* first appeared, one question seemed obvious: why Flaubert? Since he first began to worry over Flaubert, Sartre has answered the question in a variety of ways, and when volumes 1 and 2 were finally published, he took pains to give us a number of fresh and charmingly ingenuous responses (he had once made a bet with his Communist colleague Garaudy about how to approach Flaubert, the subject was well documented and therefore easy, Flaubert stands at the crossroads of all modern literary problems, etc.) whose effect, as we have seen, was to focus attention on the methodological significance and richness of his work and to minimize the importance of his own relation to Flaubert. It would seem that most of Sartre's public has refused to direct its reading of *L'Idiot* along the lines he indicated. *L'Idiot* appears to teach us as much about Sartre as it does about Flaubert, and its most intriguing problems lie in the personal origins of Sartre's fascination with Flaubert, Sartre's exorcism of his own childhood, his "envy" of Flaubert, and whether, of course, he has really succeeded in neutralizing his original antipathy for Flaubert. The third volume makes clear the limited fruitfulness of these questions, for it conveys that the personal importance of Flaubert for Sartre can only be traced to the point at which Flaubert disappears, when Sartre looks past him to his society and epoch. Nonetheless, the most intriguing problem of *L'Idiot* is still Sartre himself. Any sympathy Sartre may feel for Flaubert certainly does not extend to his society or to the literary movement Sartre claims he initiated. Volume 3 is an aggressive piece of writing, in which Sartre turns away from Flaubert only to go after bigger game.

I think it is a mistake to read *L'Idiot de la famille* as an attack on literature as a whole. Sartre's targets are broad enough without extending them: a "suspect" and "doubtful" literary doctrine, a large group of postromantic writers, an entire society. Foremost among the writers whom Sartre attacks is Mallarmé, in particular (as we have noted before) as he is the "hero and theoretician" of these writers, insofar as Sartre can make him out to be one of the last of the "knights of Nothingness."

Sartre uses this last expression ("les chevaliers du Néant") over and over, scores of times, to lend formal cohesion to the group of writers he discusses, since they are not joined together in other ways—not as a school, not politically, not as a generation, but only through aesthetic principles. He explains the idea early in his argument: in 1850, the artist writes to create a new aristocracy, knowing he lacks the tools to make himself really an aristocrat, and at the same time he writes to separate himself from humanity. He thinks of himself as either a medieval clerk or a "knight of Nothingness," someone other than human, but he is caught in an impossible circle of illogic from which there is no escape. For the sake of variety, Sartre offers us a number of versions of his formula: the Barons of Non-Humanity, the knights of Non-Being, the knights of Absolute Negation, the knights of the Imaginary and the Impossible, the misanthropes of Art-Absolute, the pioneers of Art-Neurosis, the prudent Templars of Nothingness, the Artists of Hatred. Although the irritation value of these terms may be dulled by their overuse, to a large extent they fix the belittling and negative tone of the third volume. Their ironic overtones are particularly clear to anyone who has read *Les Mots,* where Jean-Paul imagined himself a writer-knight, savior of orphan girls. In 650 pages of fairly composed exposition this stylistic tic, along with an occasional virulence of argument, stands out. It is so much in evidence, in fact, that at least once it seems to organize the text. In the second part of volume 3 ("Flaubert's neurosis and programmation: the Second Empire"), Sartre spends quite a few interesting and important pages discussing Flaubert's honorary decoration by the very government that had brought him to trial on the criminal bench. Sartre's argument is brilliant, complex, and fascinating, but it is with a certain uneasiness that one awaits his inevitable conclusion: "Flaubert is named chevalier of the Legion of Honor as he already is a chevalier of Nothingness" (574).

Perhaps Sartre can afford to play with words once or twice in 3000 pages of text. But, as much as anyone, he is aware of the defining and restricting values of repetition

and the dangers of what he once called the "trap of nomi-
nation." Why then this reliance on rhetorical abridgment,
when he is surely not so uninventive or uncritical as to be
unable to find terms that assume less? Within the massive
and forbidding armature of Sartre's methodology, these recurrent phrases provide a secondary structure of emotional
touchstones, which makes a lesser intellectual demand on
the reader but requires his complicity. The unity of the
group of writers that Sartre assembles, from Banville to
Villiers de L'Isle-Adam, from Leconte de Lisle to Mallarmé, their solidarity and reciprocal comprehension, constitute a major part of what Sartre has to prove here, but
the simple repetition of a phrase, the sealing of an idea,
makes proof seem superfluous. The act of naming itself has
a negative function in *L'Idiot,* and the cumulative effect of
this portion of the work is to give these "authors on strike"
(Mallarmé's phrase) a bad name. To pick up *L'Idiot de la
famille* intending to make one's way through its ten-page
paragraphs and two-hundred-page sections is to make a
commitment to Sartre of considerably more than just time
and effort; by the tenth, or twentieth, or fiftieth time the
reader has heard of the "knights of Nothingness," he has
got the point, and if he keeps on reading, he will most
likely do so only out of good will.

Somehow Sartre avoided this sort of thing in the first
two volumes; consequently, the parts of *L'Idiot* that deal
directly with Flaubert are much more satisfying. There is a
peculiar fascination in Sartre's immersion in Flaubertiana
—an Alice-in-Wonderland quality to the whole enterprise—
that is missing in the third volume. It is not only Sartre's
sporadically brilliant analysis of Flaubertian texts, nor his
often Byzantine usage of documentary evidence that in-
trigues, but also the compulsive force and completeness of
Flaubert's personal universe that emerge from Sartre's text,

and the way that Flaubert still slips through his fingers. In full awareness, Sartre has radicalized essential problems of biography and criticism: the superposition of one "I" upon another, the tension between a "vie romancée" and what Sartre calls a "roman vrai" (or Simone de Beauvoir, a "detective story"), the relation between imagination and documentation, individual creativity and sociohistorical determinism, verbalization and act. What he has created is a "lucid fiction," born of disrespect and fascination, which, despite its gracelessness and length, is well worth reading as an experiment in genre. But here, however much one may admire the depth of Sartre's resources, however important and controversial his theory may be, his work, as a parallel and broadened reorganization of the first two volumes, is simply less interesting.

There is a definite value in taking Flaubert at his word and holding him responsible for his hatreds, as long as Sartre remains conscious of the dangers of hyperbole and of what Flaubert called "verbalism," that is, taking the word for the thing. Sartre remains on safe ground with Flaubert because he does not equate Flaubert's misanthropy with the act of murder, but only with the dream of that act. Yet when he applies indifferently the language of pathography (l'art pour l'art implies the "hysterical imitation of a schizophrenic world view") to *all* the writers of 1850, when he evokes genocide as their common goal, his work emerges as the opposite of a hagiography: an accounting of the lives of sinners (hamartiography?), or of the damned, if you will. Sartre can hardly avoid giving names to the artists he treats, and he does so with Flaubert: "prince of recrimination," "flower of lesser evil," "family idiot," and so on. But the negative act of naming Flaubert is always framed within Sartre's more profound ambivalence toward him. Not so with the "knights of

Nothingness." Leconte de Lisle, for example, to whom
Sartre devotes one hundred pages, is a "pisse-froid," too
stupid and empty to equal Flaubert in any way, a fake
Vigny, false noble and false misanthrope, a contagious
madman, and nothing more.

On the whole, Sartre's tastes have remained remarkably
constant over the years. He dislikes Leconte de Lisle and
the Goncourts, he approves of Hugo (because he is read by
the working class) and the Communard Courbet, and if he
no longer bothers to attack Bourget and Barrès, it is only
because he has found a more worthy adversary in Mallarmé.
In volume 3 he retouches both *Saint Genet* (how can a
"black" writer have universal import?) and *Baudelaire,* but
the basic tone of his animadversions goes even further back
to the first essays gathered in *Situations.* As we have seen,
his hero was there the courageous phenomenologist, man
among men, who penetrated into reality and accepted its
horror and charm; his villain was a docile, passive observer
of reality, "bavard de salon," who hid from reality in the
humid world of his dreams. In Sartre's first critical works,
it was always clear that writing should be an act, that the
idea took precedence over its expression, and that the purpose of literature was to communicate truth—the writer
should have something to say. Between 1850 and 1870,
however, according to Sartre in *L'Idiot,* fiction is not communication but its opposite: "To write is to speak with
nothing to say, as one does in the salons" (301). The great
writers of the time have "profound intuitions, and admi-
rable comprehension of certain forms of behavior and
certain attitudes" (322), but hate and scorn deform their
work. They are the contrary of men of action; their
writing seeks in no way to provoke the reader into taking a
moral position nor does it seek to convey the truth, but
rather to express "the fable of the world."

What has changed is Sartre's idea of truth. We have seen that there has always been an underlying self-accusation in Sartre's criticism: to write is to falsify a primitive totalizing intuition of the world; the writer and the intellectual are traitors. In the early essays this guilt was reflected mostly in a dislike for literary "chatter": he deemed Nabokov too self-conscious, too well read, Faulkner too wordy, and he thought that where possible the most concise form of expression was the best. Concision, economy, immediacy: bygone virtues. With the development of contemporary forms of criticism and the novel, and since *Les Mots,* Sartre has turned more and more to the idea of writing as a self-reflective act. Exhaustive discourse cannot express everything; "total truth is necessarily poetry" (337). If so, unless *L'Idiot de la famille* can be considered the poem of Flaubert's life, one can hardly expect even 3000 pages of "literary" prose to give us Flaubert's irreducible truth, and *L'Idiot* contains its own self-criticism.

If we read *L'Idiot* as a novel, as Sartre has asked us to, then it is a novel not only about Flaubert and Sartre, but also about language and the act of writing, and its creative impulse is carried in the search for a new prose form. In his article on André Gorz, Sartre recalled that, as a child, when he talked too much, his parents would say, "Be still, you stream of warm water!" (Quand je faisais le bavard, on me disait: 'Tais-toi, filet d'eau tiède.') Since his childhood, Sartre has conceived of language as a warm, wet flow, a stream in which man bathes, just as he is immersed in his blood and his sperm. As the presence of the other can be a warm, englobing atmosphere, an inauthentic womb around the individual, so the brute power of words can be caught in a trembling, inconsistent jelly of socialized usages and poetic resonances. The sharp edges of a language of action or a language of values can be blunted by the material accidents of connotation and association; poetry, except as it is directed by an explosive masculine genius, appears as a threat to communicative language and its function of remaking society, in the same way that an amorphous, feminine world of vegetation and flesh once seemed to menace Sartre himself.

This idea has been at the core of Sartre's writing and criticism from the beginning. From his childhood, he has sought direction and definition in a shapeless world through language, that is, through a medium he considers as neutral and flaccid as the world itself. But to find the truth, to comprehend the freaks of chance, Sartre has found no tool but language. Writing, then, had somehow to be his salvation; it was to be a sword "as hard and beautiful as steel," slashing through the dark night toward the light. The artist's task was to cleanse language, as the goal of art was to purify existence: through language, Sartre could rid himself of a personal and political guilt; he could refuse to accept the world in a way that might change the world.

Although all art is essentially unification and ordering, for Sartre, its only immediately viable form is one that first accepts disorder and disunity in order to transcend them. In a large part of his criticism, art is related to violence; most authentically, for Sartre, literature is a dry, sudden attack on a feminine society, and style, properly conceived of, is a weapon. The urge toward precision and shape in Sartre is countered by a denial of spiritless orderliness. His aesthetic order is an order of violence, an explosion of words thrown pell-mell outwards and up. The contradictory forces within the writer, multiplied and objectified in art, can be welded together, concentrated, in the "false unity of the Word" only in provisional spirals

that always break free and forward. The writer thrusts
ahead to find a self always fleeing before him.

The best in Sartre's criticism has never been born of his
adherence to method, but in the force of poetic vision that
passes beyond dogmatism. Neither the majority of the
early essays in *Situations,* where the writer in Sartre is
frequently subordinate to the philosopher, nor *Baudelaire,*
conceived in antipathy, will live on as great criticism, while
Saint Genet will, in all likelihood. Whether or not one believes in the Jean Genet Sartre portrays, *Saint Genet* forces
itself forward with a sweeping thrust of creative energy
and urgency that makes it much harder to dismiss than
Baudelaire.

But one cannot measure *L'Idiot de la famille* in the same
terms. Sartre's critical problem, as we have understood it,
is to find definition through a pale and formless linguistic
instrument. Through the rhetoric and fiction of *Baudelaire,*
"Orphée noir," and *Saint Genet,* he sharpened one set of
stylistic weapons to a fine point of precision, and every
broadening of method only added weight to his attack. By
L'Idiot, he has understood that the weapon he employs is
inadequate to man's situation: it was constructed on the
illusion of not being illusion. *L'Idiot de la famille* recognizes the holes in language, the poetically attainable sense
beyond the page in each work of literature, and admits the
validity of the indirect and the formal in style. Sartre apparently now considers a violently direct approach to
language and self-definition as futile; though the writer
communicates transcendent values and ideas, the authenticity of his writing is as much a peripheral matter of style
as it is directness of thought. Ideas are still to be preferred
to words, but meanings are no longer thought to be so
easily controlled. Sartre sees that style condenses a whole

man, an entire life; it reflects an original choice evident
even in its denial. So, the verbal release and looseness of
L'Idiot represent, on one level, a conscious and controlled
surrender to what Sartre likes to think of as the limp flow
and vague passiveness of language, a surrender to (Sartre's)
Flaubert in the name of order on an immense scale.

At the same time, in *L'Idiot*, Sartre's basic message remains unchanged. The dialectics of sexuality, of form and
matter, reality and dream, metaphysics and technique,
passivity and activity, pathos and praxis, solitude and
communion, silence and language, *dire* and *manière de
dire*, are maneuvered and adjusted around his earlier theory
of writing as a masculine act of heroism and aggression.
Sartre denies the heroic role of criticism on one level to
reaffirm on another the ultimately virile nature of literature. He no longer seems so concerned with the self he
sought to define, nor with the childhood he once rejected;
he is willing to let the self be invented through another.

Through empathy he reaches for a new prose form,
which he perceives as a negation and reconstruction of his
previous work. His early critical essays are, relatively, rigid
constructs, unchangeable and set, once conceived. They
imply little openness to facts or willingness to change, to
retotalize, interpretation through the addition of new
facts. The new form of Sartre's criticism is based on the
rejection of criticism as a closed construct. He aims, then,
at a comprehensively ordered form through a continually
changing point of view, through the disorder of words and
the disorder of the self; he creates a form both tighter and
looser than his early works, truly a critical fiction that expresses two opposing directions of Sartre's project. On the
one hand, Sartre has never ceased striving to make himself
into a steely, silent, and manly hero of literature and

philosophy; on the other, he is always drawn back to art to make of himself a complete and integrated creator. *Les Mots* celebrated the murder of the poetic, infantile artist and the suicide of the heroic artist in Sartre; in *L'Idiot de la famille*, between the lines, both are reborn.

Selected Bibliography

Works of Jean-Paul Sartre Cited in the Text

A. French

Sartre, Jean-Paul. *Baudelaire*. Paris: Gallimard, 1947.

———. *Les Chemins de la liberté*. Paris: Gallimard, 1945–49.

———. *Critique de la raison dialectique*. Paris: Gallimard (Bibliothèque des Idées), 1960.

———. "Un Entretien avec Jean-Paul Sartre." *Le Monde*, May 14, 1971, pp. 17–21.

———. *L'Etre et le Néant, essai de phénoménologie ontologique*. Paris: Gallimard (Bibliothèque des Idées), 1943.

———. *L'Idiot de la famille. Gustave Flaubert de 1821 à 1857*. Paris: Gallimard (Bibliothèque de Philosophie), vols. 1 & 2, 1971, vol. 3, 1972.

———. *L'Imaginaire, psychologie phénoménologique de l'imagination*. Paris: Gallimard, 1940.

———. *L'Imagination*. Paris: Presses Universitaires de France, 1969. Original publication: Paris: Librairie Félix Alcan, 1936.

———. *Les Mots*. Paris: Gallimard, 1964.

———. *Les Mouches*. Paris: Gallimard, 1944.

———. *La Nausée*. Paris: Gallimard, 1938.

———. *Plaidoyer pour les intellectuels*. Paris: Gallimard (Bibliothèque des Idées), 1972.

———. *Questions de méthode*. Paris: Gallimard (Bibliothèque des Idées), 1960.

———. *Saint Genet, Comédien et martyr*. Paris: Gallimard, 1952.

———. *Situations*. Paris: Gallimard.

> Vol. 1: 1947.
> Vol. 2: 1948.
> Vol. 3: 1949.
> Vol. 4: Portraits, 1964.
> Vol. 9: Mélanges, 1972.

——. *Un Théâtre de Situations*. Paris: Gallimard (Bibliothèque des Idées), 1971.

B. In Translation

——. *Baudelaire*, translated by Martin Turnell, Norfolk, Conn.: James Laughlin, 1950.

——. *Being and Nothingness*, translated by Hazel E. Barnes. New York: Washington Square Press, 1953.

——. *Black Orpheus*, translated by S. W. Allen. Présence Africaine, n.d.

——. *Politics and Literature*, translated by J. A. Underwood and John Calder. London: Calder and Boyars, 1973.

——. *The Psychology of Imagination*, translated by Bernard Frechtman. New York: Washington Square Press, 1968.

——. *Saint Genet, Actor and Martyr*, translated by Bernard Frechtman. New York: Braziller, 1963.

——. *Search for a Method*, translated by Hazel E. Barnes. New York: Knopf, 1963.

——. *Situations*, translated by Benita Eisler. New York: Braziller, 1965.

——. *What Is Literature?*, translated by Bernard Frechtman. New York: Washington Square Press, 1966.

——. *The Words*, translated by Bernard Frechtman. New York: Braziller, 1964.

Secondary Works

Arnold, A. James, and Piriou, Jean-Pierre. *Genèse et critique d'une autobiographie: Les Mots de Sartre*. Paris: Minard, 1973.

Audry, Colette. *Sartre*. Paris: Seghers, 1966.

Barnes, Hazel E. *Sartre*. Philadelphia: Lippincott, 1973.

Bauer, George H. *Sartre and the Artist*. Chicago: University of Chicago Press, 1969.

Beauvoir, Simone de. *Le Deuxième Sexe*. Paris: Gallimard, 1949.

——. *La Force de l'âge*. Paris: Gallimard, 1960.

——. *La Force des choses*. Paris: Gallimard, 1963.

——. *Tout Compte fait*. Paris: Gallimard, 1972.

Blanchot, Maurice. "L'échec de Baudelaire." *L'Arche* 3, no. 24 (February, 1947): 80–91.

——. *La Part du feu.* Paris: Gallimard, 1949.

Brée, Germaine. *Camus and Sartre: Crisis and Commitment.* New York: Delacorte Press, 1972.

Brombert, Victor. *The Intellectual Hero.* Philadelphia: Lippincott, 1961.

Champigny, Robert. "Langage et littérature selon Sartre." *Revue d'Esthétique* 19, fasc. 2 (April–June, 1966): 131–48.

——. *Pour une Esthétique de l'essai.* Paris: Minard, 1967.

——. "Trying to Understand L'*Idiot.*" *Diacritics* 2, no. 2 (Summer, 1972): 2–6.

Cohn, Robert G. "Sartre vs. Proust." *Partisan Review* 28, nos. 5–6 (1961): 633–45.

Contat, Michel. "Sartre at Seventy: An Interview." *New York Review* 22, no. 13 (August 7, 1975): 10–17.

Contat, Michel, and Rybalka, Michel. *Les Ecrits de Sartre.* Paris: Gallimard, 1970.

Les Critiques de notre temps et Sartre. Paris: Garnier, 1972.

Desan, Wilfred. *The Marxism of Jean-Paul Sartre.* New York: Doubleday, Anchor Books, 1966.

Diéguez, Manuel de. *L'Ecrivain et son langage.* Paris: Gallimard, 1962.

Elevitch, Bernard. "Sartre and Genet." *Massachusetts Review* 5 (Winter, 1964): 408–13.

Grene, Marjorie. *Sartre.* New York: New Viewpoints, 1973.

Hahn, Otto. "L'Oeuvre critique de Sartre," *Modern Language Notes* 80, no. 3 (May, 1965): 347–63.

Hardré, Jacques. "Jean-Paul Sartre: Literary Critic." *Studies in Philology* 40, no. 1 (January, 1958): 98–106.

Isère, Jean. "Ambiguïté de l'Esthétique de Sartre." *French Review* 21 (March, 1948): 357–60.

——. "Sartre vs. Proust," *Kenyon Review* 9 (1947): 287–89.

Jameson, Fredric. *Sartre: The Origins of a Style.* New Haven: Yale University Press, 1961).

——. *Marxism and Form.* Princeton: Princeton University Press, 1971.

——. "Three Methods in Sartre's Literary Criticism." In *Modern French Criticism,* edited by John K. Simon, pp. 193–228. Chicago: University of Chicago Press, 1972.

Jeanson, Francis. *Le Problème moral de la pensée de Sartre.* Paris: Editions du Myrte, 1947.

——. *Sartre par lui-même.* Paris: Editions de Seuil, 1969.

——. *Sartre dans sa vie.* Paris: Editions de Seuil, 1974.

Jourdain, Louis. "Sartre devant Baudelaire." *Tel Quel* 19 (Autumn, 1964): 70–85; 21 (Spring, 1965): 79–95.

Kaelin, Eugene. *An Existentialist Aesthetic: The Theories of Sartre and Merleau-Ponty.* Madison: The University of Wisconsin Press, 1962.

Kern, Edith, ed. *Sartre: A Collection of Critical Essays.* Englewood Cliffs, New Jersey: Prentice-Hall, 1962.

Laing, R. D., and Cooper, D. G. *Reason and Violence: A Decade of Sartre's Philosophy, 1950–1960.* London: Tavistock Publications, 1964.

Laufer, Roger. "Sartre as a Literary Critic." *Meanjin,* Winter, 1959, pp. 427–34.

Leiris, Michel. *Brisées.* Paris: Mercure de France, 1966.

Lesage, Laurent. *The French New Criticism.* University Park, Pa.: Penn State University Press, 1967.

Levin, Harry. "A Literary Enormity: Sartre on Flaubert." *Journal of the History of Ideas* 23, no. 4 (October–December, 1972): 643–49.

Lilar, Suzanne. *A propos de Sartre et de l'amour.* Paris: Grasset, 1967.

MacMahon, Joseph. *Humans Being: The World of Jean-Paul Sartre.* Chicago: University of Chicago Press, 1971.

Manser, Anthony. *Sartre: A Philosophic Study.* London: Athlone Press, 1966.

Mehlman, Jeffrey. *A Structural Study of Autobiography.* Ithaca: Cornell University Press, 1974.

Mouchard, Claude. "Un roman vrai?" *Critique,* no. 295 (December, 1971), pp. 1029–49.

Murdock, Iris. *Sartre: Romantic Rationalist.* New Haven: Yale University Press, 1953.

Paulhan, Jean. "Jean-Paul Sartre n'est pas en bons termes avec les mots." *Table Ronde,* November, 1950, pp. 9–20.

Peyre, Henri. *Jean-Paul Sartre.* New York: Columbia University Press, 1968.

Que peut la littérature? Paris: L'Inédit (10/18), 1965.

Rau, Catherine. "The Aesthetic Views of Jean-Paul Sartre." *Journal of Aesthetics and Art Criticism* 9, no. 2 (December, 1950): 139–48.

St. Aubyn, F. C. "Sartre and the Essential Genet," *Symposium* 8, no. 1 (Summer, 1954): 82–101.

Sartre aujourd'hui. L'Arc no. 30. Aix-en-Provence, 1966.

Sheridan, James Francis. *Sartre: The Radical Conversion.* Athens, Ohio: Ohio University Press, 1969.

Suhl, Benjamin. *Jean-Paul Sartre: The Philosopher as a Literary Critic.* New York: Columbia University Press, 1971.

Thody, Philip. *Jean-Paul Sartre: A Literary and Political Study.* New York: Macmillan, 1960.

——. "Jean-Paul Sartre as a Literary Critic." *The London Magazine,* November, 1960, pp. 61-64.

——. *Sartre: A Biographical Introduction.* London: Studio Vista, 1971.

Ungar, Steven R. "Sartre as Critic." *Diacritics* 1, no. 1 (Fall, 1971): 32-37.

——. "Sartre, Ponge and the Ghost of Husserl." *Substance* 8 (Winter, 1974): 139-50.

Verstraeten, Pierre. *Violence et éthique.* Paris: Gallimard, 1972.

Warnock, Mary, ed. *Sartre: A Collection of Critical Essays.* Garden City, New York: Doubleday, Anchor Books, 1971.

Yale French Studies no. 30. New Haven, 1963.

Zimmerman, Eugenia J. *Metaphysics and Technique in the Expository Prose of Jean-Paul Sartre, 1936-1960.* Ann Arbor: University Microfilms, 1965.

Index